Young Nietzsche and the Wagnerian Experience

UNC | COLLEGE OF ARTS AND SCIENCES
Germanic and Slavic Languages and Literatures

From 1949 to 2004, UNC Press and the UNC Department of Germanic & Slavic Languages and Literatures published the UNC Studies in the Germanic Languages and Literatures series. Monographs, anthologies, and critical editions in the series covered an array of topics including medieval and modern literature, theater, linguistics, philology, onomastics, and the history of ideas. Through the generous support of the National Endowment for the Humanities and the Andrew W. Mellon Foundation, books in the series have been reissued in new paperback and open access digital editions. For a complete list of books visit www.uncpress.org.

Young Nietzsche and the Wagnerian Experience

FREDERICK R. LOVE

UNC Studies in the Germanic Languages and Literatures
Number 39

Copyright © 1963

This work is licensed under a Creative Commons CC BY-NC-ND license. To view a copy of the license, visit http://creativecommons.org/licenses.

Suggested citation: Love, Frederick R. *Young Nietzsche and the Wagnerian Experience*. Chapel Hill: University of North Carolina Press, 1963. DOI: https://doi.org/10.5149/9781469657837_Love

Library of Congress Cataloging-in-Publication Data
Names: Love, Frederick R.
Title: Young Nietzsche and the Wagnerian experience / by Frederick R. Love.
Other titles: University of North Carolina Studies in the Germanic Languages and Literatures ; no. 39.
Description: Chapel Hill : University of North Carolina Press, [1963] Series: University of North Carolina Studies in the Germanic Languages and Literatures. | Includes bibliographical references.
Identifiers: LCCN 63063585 | ISBN 978-0-8078-8039-5 (pbk: alk. paper) | ISBN 978-1-4696-5783-7 (ebook)
Subjects: Nietzsche, Friedrich Wilhelm, 1844-1900. | Wagner, Richard, 1813-1883.
Classification: LCC PD25 .N6 NO. 39

PREFACE

To many a reader it will scarcely seem necessary to add another study to the sizable literature on Nietzsche and Wagner. That was indeed my own view when I began an investigation of Nietzsche's relation to music and musicians after the break with Wagner – in the period of his mature philosophy. Yet even in this context I was repeatedly confronted with questions as to Nietzsche's native musical talent, his early training, and the changing musical preferences of his youth. The question of his affinity for Wagnerian music seemed on closer examination to have no simple answer, and the role of the writings of Hanslick and Schopenhauer in shaping his musical opinions or guiding his tastes had never been adequately discussed. Moreover the chief witness to Nietzsche's early development, his sister Elisabeth, had chosen to disregard the possibility of an influence exerted on him by musical friends and acquaintances.

On the basis of earlier studies, the latest published source material, and a sampling of Nietzsche's unpublished compositions, it was possible to deal with these problems at least in a preliminary way. In the matter of the philosopher's early relation to Wagnerian music, however, it seemed clear that more decisive results were to be obtained if the unpublished musical manuscripts could be studied in greater continuity than was feasible at the time.

Through the cooperation of various archives and kind individuals I was subsequently able to eliminate the important gaps in my knowledge of Nietzsche's musical production, and in this I was substantially aided during a visit to Weimar in the summer of 1959. In addition to furnishing first hand evidence of his musical talent and judgment, the record of Nietzsche's compositions clearly provides a basis for modifying the widely held view of the philosopher as a passionate devotee of Wagnerian music.

While it does not actually form the center of the present monograph, the study of this body of new material is its primary justification. The results are coordinated with a careful analysis of the published sources, wherein previously overlooked clues have in some cases led to new information relevant to Nietzsche's intellectual development. Virtually all sources now available or likely to become generally available have been exploited in the attempt to illuminate the problematic nature of Nietzsche's Wagnerian experience.

I would here like to express my gratitude to the following individuals and institutions for their help in making available the manuscripts essential to this study: Professor Alfred Cortot, Lausanne, Dr. Joachim Bergfeld, Director of the Museum und Archiv, Richard Wagner-Gedenkstätte der Stadt Bayreuth, Dr. Max Burckhardt, Curator of Manuscripts at the Öffentliche Bibliothek der Universität Basel, and Dr. Karl-Heinz Hahn, Director of the Goethe- und Schiller-Archiv, Weimar.

FREDERICK R. LOVE

Brown University
Providence, R. I.
Spring, 1962

TABLE OF CONTENTS

Preface	VII
List of Abbreviations	XI
Young Nietzsche and the Wagnerian Experience	1
Introduction	1
I From Naumburg to Pforta	4
II Music and the Creative Impulse	19
III The Aesthetic Problem of the New Music	31
IV Music and Metaphysics	37
V The Master Singer	51
VI "Der Melomane"	67
VII Rupture	77
Notes	85
List of Works Cited	95
Index	99

LIST OF ABBREVIATIONS

I-XVI. Otherwise unidentified Roman numerals refer to the volumes of Friędrich Nietzsche, *Werke*, Leipzig: C. G. Naumann and A. Kröner, 1901-11.

GB I-V. Friedrich Nietzsche, *Gesammelte Briefe*, 5 vols. Berlin and Leipzig, 1900-09.

Hanslick. Eduard Hanslick, *Vom Musikalisch-Schönen*, 3d ed., Leipzig, 1865.

HK I-V. Friedrich Nietzsche, *Werke: Historisch-kritische Gesamtausgabe*, 5 vols. Munich, 1934-40.

HKB I-IV. Friedrich Nietzsche, *Briefe: Historisch-kritische Gesamtausgabe*, 4 vols. Munich, 1938-42.

Leben I-III. Elisabeth Förster-Nietzsche, *Das Leben Friedrich Nietzsches*, 3 vols. Leipzig, 1895-1904.

Newman I-IV. Ernest Newman, *The Life of Richard Wagner*, 4 vols. New York, 1933-46.

NZfM. *Neue Zeitschrift für Musik*, ed. Robert Schumann, Franz Brendel, *et al.*, Leipzig, 1834 ff.

Schlechta I-III. Friedrich Nietzsche, *Werke in drei Bänden*, ed. Karl Schlechta, 3 vols. Munich, 1956.

INTRODUCTION

During the productive euphoria of his last autumn in Turin, Nietzsche celebrated in his autobiographical *Ecce homo* one of the most significant episodes in his spiritual development, characterizing his early relationship to Wagnerian music in a few deft strokes:

> Von dem Augenblick an, wo es einen Klavierauszug des Tristan gab – mein Compliment, Herr von Bülow! – war ich Wagnerianer. Die älteren Werke Wagner's sah ich unter mir – noch zu gemein, zu "deutsch"... Aber ich suche heute noch nach einem Werke von gleich gefährlicher Fascination, von einer gleich schauerlichen und süßen Unendlichkeit, wie der Tristan ist, – ich suche in allen Künsten vergebens. (XV, 39)[1]

The moment recalled was the spring of 1861, when Nietzsche was not yet seventeen years old and in his third year at the respected old academy of Schulpforta. Nearly eight years later and less than a month after his first personal encounter with Wagner, he described this composer in a letter to his friend Erwin Rohde as "ein Genius ... der mir wie ein unlösliches Problem erschien und zu dessen Verständnis ich Jahr aus Jahr ein neue Anläufe machte..." (GB II, 110; HKB II, 279-280).

Clearly the contrast between these two statements suggests a serious discrepancy in Nietzsche's later account and emphasizes once again the need for caution in accepting at face value some of the dramatic formulations found in the "symbolic" autobiography. Indeed this particular inconsistency has not escaped the notice of recent scholars;[2] however no one has yet undertaken a fresh analysis of this early period in Nietzsche's musical experience. Surely this is due in part to the scanty documentation and the presence of apparent contradictions even within this small body of evidence. Furthermore any serious attempt at clarification of Nietzsche's early relationship to Wagnerian music must inevitably make its terms with the account of the most voluble witness of these early years, Frau Förster-Nietzsche, who maintained that her brother had been converted to Wagnerian music even prior to the existence of Bülow's piano arrangement of the *Tristan* music (*Leben* I, 135).

There has never been a dearth of writers eager to discuss Nietzsche's friendship with and subsequent alienation from Wagner; to date these have been explained from almost every conceivable point of view and have been made to furnish evidence for any number of cultural analyses of the nineteenth century, for which Nietzsche's own interpretation merely set the example. The years leading up to this friendship have either been neglected altogether or dispatched with a few generalizations deriving from the image in *Ecce homo*. Yet it seems clear that a successful investigation of this formative period in Nietzsche's development should offer a better perspective from which to interpret the Wagnerian episode of his youth and the musical problem in general as it is mani-

INTRODUCTION

fested during his philosophically productive years.

Surviving literary documents of the earliest period have been published with admirable care and thoroughness by the editors of the interrupted *Historisch-kritische Gesamtausgabe* and have thus been available for more than twenty years. If we assume that no further information of this type will come to light, the only reasonable way of expanding the base of such an investigation would be to consider the extant musical sketches and compositions dating from these years, of which only a small fraction was ever published.[3] The present writer has succeeded in gaining access to almost all of Nietzsche's remaining musical manuscripts, the analysis of which not only yields a clear picture of his gifts, his training and his independent musical achievements, but also provides evidence of the shifting musical influences upon him, including that of Wagner. In large measure the consideration of Nietzsche's approach to Wagnerian music must remain involved with that of his total musical experience, aspects of which will be unfamiliar even to specialists. Hence the analysis below of necessity becomes broader at times than its title might indicate.

I. FROM NAUMBURG TO PFORTA

Obviously the limits set for this study forbid a complete recapitulation of the details of Nietzsche's earliest exposures to music, for which the HK provides us with many clues; but the main events retold here are characteristic. As a child he had a high degree of responsiveness to music and to aural impressions as such, well demonstrated in an incident dating from his fourth year. It scarcely seems mere coincidence for the later admirer of *Tristan und Isolde* that music and death were so inextricably part of the same childhood experience. At the funeral services for his father it was the tolling of the bells and the solemn pealing of the organ which made the deepest impression on him. Later, we are told, this same music formed the accompaniment to an uncannily prophetic dream of the death of his small brother (HK I, 5-6). Nietzsche's various autobiographical sketches further show that it was also a musical experience which released the initial creative impulse in the young boy, this time identified in one of the accounts as the "Hallelujah Chorus" from the *Messiah* (HK I, 18).

> Durch einen besonderen Zufall aufgeweckt begann ich im 9t. Jahre leidenschaftlich die Musik und zwar sogleich componierend, wenn anders man die Bemühungen des erregten Kindes, zusammenklingende und -folgende Töne zu Papier zu bringen und biblische Texte mit einer phantastischen Begleitung des Pianoforte abzusingen, componieren nennen kann. (HK III, 67)

FROM NAUMBURG TO PFORTA

There is no reliable evidence that Nietzsche had enjoyed any formal training in music up to this moment – which seems curious enough in view of the almost inevitable union of music and theology in the Protestant parsonages of Germany – and no subsequent information suggests that the boy's grounding in music was either thorough or sustained. In musical matters Nietzsche remained largely self-taught, and the sole reference to a teacher in all of the autobiographical material is an unenthusiastic recollection of his first year at the *Gymnasium* in Naumburg.

> Insbesondere keimte damals die Neigung zur Musik, trotzdem daß die Anfänge des Unterrichts ganz danach angetan waren, sie in der Wurzel zu vernichten. Mein erster Lehrer war nämlich ein Kantor, behaftet mit allen liebenswürdigen Fehlern eines Kantors, und dazu eines emeritierten ohne besondere Verdienste.
> (Schlechta III, 109)

Wherever the formal instruction was found wanting or even lacking altogether, Nietzsche's own enthusiasm and talent tended to compensate; for he learned to read music and play at sight, he explored the musical literature available to him in piano arrangements, and – like his father before him – developed a facility in free improvisation at the keyboard which was at least admired by many of his less critical schoolmates and companions. Composition seemed to be a response to a natural urge, but in the absence of any rigorous study of the traditional techniques of the art, his efforts often bore a striking resemblance to free improvisations. Nietzsche's creativity in a musical sphere was doubtless a beneficial outlet for a highly excitable youngster, and it remained a more direct and satisfying mode of self-expression than he could attain in a literary sense for yet some time to come. He developed no particularly high degree of technical proficiency as a pianist; the extensive literature for the keyboard did not interest him. In the illuminating "practice lists" we find the easier Beethoven sonatas, the simpler pieces of Bach and Schubert, and beyond this mainly the various arrangements of choral and orchestral music made more for study than performance.

In the absence of professional guidance in music it is not surprising that the influence of musical friends in Naumburg on the young Nietzsche became all the more significant. By far the most important of his early friendships in this respect was that with Gustav Krug, a relationship which Frau Förster-Nietzsche generally preferred to slight, presumably for the greater glory of her brother. Krug was the son of an accomplished amateur musician who was in social contact with some of the musical luminaries of the day, a group including musicians of the stature of Felix Mendelssohn (HK I, 12). Young Krug in turn enjoyed in his musical education all the thoroughness which Nietzsche lacked, and the Lieder which he later published reveal an honest craftsman with advanced late-romantic harmonic tendencies.[4] Frequent musical soirées in the Krug home were governed by the conservative tastes of Geheimrat Krug, but this household was by no means as impervious to modern influences as Frau Förster-Nietzsche would have us believe. Young Nietzsche seems rather to have developed a dogmatic conservatism out of his own musical experiments.

> Ich empfing dadurch auch einen unauslöschlichen Haß gegen alle moderne Musik und alles, was nicht klassisch war. Mozart und Haidn [*sic*], Schubert und Mendelsohn Beethoven und Bach das sind die Säulen auf die sich nur deutsche Musik und ich gründete. (HK I, 18)

When this was written (1858) Nietzsche had little use for the "Zukunftsmusik" of a Liszt or a Berlioz, unappealing as it was to "das gesunde Menschenohr" (HK I, 27), and Wagner he did not mention at all. As one might have expected from his pious family background he condemned all ostentatious or frivolous music (HK I, 27) and defended the oratorio as a musical genre superior to the opera well into the early days of his acquaintance with Wagnerian music (cf. HKB I, 125). Involved were not only moral reasons but also the recognition that the oratorio was essentially absolute music, despite its adherence to a text. In January 1861 he expounded this view in a letter to his friends Krug and Pinder:

> So verschmäht das Oratorium alle andern Mittel, deren sich die Oper zur Wirkung bedient; es kann von niemand für etwas Begleitendes wie die Opernmusik doch für die Menge noch ist, gehalten werden. Kein andrer Sinn wird hier erregt außer dem Gehör. (HKB I, 125)

Characteristically Nietzsche objected to the artificiality of the *recitativo secco* as employed in the traditional oratorio, a point of coincidental agreement with Wagnerian theory. But whereas Wagner abominated the genre altogether,[5] Nietzsche merely wished to "modernize" it by the substitution of spoken melodrama between the set arias and choruses. In fact *Oper und Drama*, which contained the details of Wagner's plans for reforming the opera, was unknown to Nietzsche until some years later.[6] He was however not ignorant of the general tenor of the new theories in the early 1860's, as is shown in the occasional references to Wagner in letters and notes of this period. But his immediate interest in the last years at Schulpforta was concentrated on a romantic composer already dead: Robert Schumann. In the same manner in which he had earlier studied the available scores of Haydn, Mozart and Beethoven, he now sought to absorb the orchestral and choral works of Schumann; even the university student in Leipzig still took special delight in this music (*cf.* HKB II, 45). Yet the intervening years had also given him opportunity to become familiar with a considerable sampling of the music of

Berlioz, Liszt and Wagner, not to mention the "moderns" of lesser stature. To a marked degree Nietzsche's old intolerance had been dissipated, but no revolution in his taste had taken place.

The broadening of his musical interests from the narrowly classical toward the most recent trends can be observed particularly well in two related activities of the years at Pforta. His participation in an intellectual forum known as the "Germania" with two of his old schoolmates is well documented, and this information is supplemented by the testimony of his own compositions of the same period. From his earliest schooldays in Naumburg Nietzsche had been fortunate enough to have two congenial friends with whom he could share his youthful enthusiasm for music and literature: Gustav Krug, known to us already, and Wilhelm Pinder, who had developed an especial attachment to literature while sharing in the musical interests of the other two. The association with Krug had been profitable for Nietzsche musically from the outset of their acquaintance. However the sharing of cultural experiences had been on a completely informal basis and the relationship would normally have deteriorated when Nietzsche transferred from the *Gymnasium* at Naumburg to the boarding school Schulpforta in 1858, had it not been for an active correspondence and their common activities during vacation time. In July of 1860 they agreed to formalize their efforts in the founding of the "Germania," a monthly forum requiring essayistic, poetical or musical contributions from the three members. To enable the club to purchase books and music there were to be regular dues, and fines were to be imposed for infraction of club regulations; in order to impress further upon the members the seriousness of their commitments there were appropriately solemn inaugural ceremonies in the tower of a nearby ruined castle. Since the affairs of the "Germania" were carried on over the distance between Naumburg and Schulpforta, there is rather more documentation of its proceedings than might otherwise be the case. For the most part, the monthly contributions were passed around and subjected to written criticisms by the others; but four times a year, during vacations, the members read or performed their works before the assembled body, or "Synod." The office of chronicler for the club rotated quarterly, and it was the duty of the chronicler at each synod meeting to give a digest of criticisms offered since the previous session.

Needless to say, the "Germania" did not always function smoothly, but the organization was active for three full years, or until its members became engrossed in preparation for their comprehensive school examinations. In the summer of 1862, when delinquency of the members in submitting their contributions and an impoverished treasury threatened the existence of the club, it was Nietzsche in his function as chronicler who put the "Germania" back on its feet. There is ample reason to credit him also with being the prime mover in this club founded on such excellent pedagogical principles;

it was he who constantly kept before the members both the goals of their undertaking and a view of their past achievements. In addition to his vigorous address to the improvised synod meeting of September 1862, Nietzsche made a study of the first twenty-five months of the club's operation and provided a complete index of the literary and musical contributions during that period. In his address he called for the prompt fulfillment of all overdue obligations and a tightening of the club's regulations. Then he proposed a general essay contest on a theme of common interest ("Über das Wesen der Musik") so as to revive the competitive intellectual climate and counteract the "Verdumpfung und Versumpfung unsrer Germania" (HK II, 92).

Particularly useful to the historian is the index of contributions made by Nietzsche in his survey as well as the supplement of June 1863 (HK II, 220). Fully half of his own contributions were musical or relevant to music, and some fourteen of these were actual compositions. In this field he vied with Krug and in the realm of poetry with Pinder. All three in their essayistic discourses from time to time concerned themselves with the problem of music in its relation to poetry and drama. Yet far from demonstrating leadership in this department, which unavoidably touched on the Wagnerian innovations, Nietzsche was the least communicative of the three; Krug delivered at least three reports or essays on Wagnerian music and another on modern musical trends in general, and Pinder became embroiled in arguments with him over the relationship of word and tone and the problem of "Das Kunstwerk der Zukunft." For Krug and Pinder, it is true, these arguments were more in the nature of sport than of serious contention. Thus Krug would counter friend Pinder's assertions either with Wagnerian or anti-Wagnerian arguments, whichever scored for him at the particular moment (cf. HK II, 439-441). In all of this Nietzsche remained strikingly reticent; it was still the oratorio which concerned him more than any self-consciously "dramatic" music – an interest evident in both his essays and his musical compositions for the "Germania."

During the spring vacation of 1861 Krug and Nietzsche had the opportunity of previewing the new piano-vocal score of *Tristan und Isolde* by Hans von Bülow, a privilege apparently enjoyed through the elder Krug's connections with music publishers. How the reactions of the two "musicians" of the "Germania" differed is clearly discernible in Krug's subsequent letter to Nietzsche, whose own comments have unfortunately not survived. Before returning the score Krug studied the entire work, and his remarks are unmistakably those of the proselytizer:

> Gleich nach dem Ende der Ferien schickte ich Tristan und Isolde wieder zurück, von dem Du leider ungefähr nur die Hälfte gehört hast. Gerade der 2te und 3te Akt sind wunderschön, obgleich der 2te anfangs nicht recht verständ-

> lich ist und etwas ermüdet. Bei mehrmaligem Hören aber erkennt man erst die großen Schönheiten und man könnte wohl sagen, daß der 2te Akt den Culminationspunkt der Oper bildet. (HKB I, 368)

Krug was understandably excited by the possibility that *Tristan* might be performed at the coming *Tonkünstlerversammlung* in Weimar (HKB I, 368), and would gladly have made the trip there with his friend; but as was so often the case with this work, hopes for an early production came to nought (premiere in 1865). Nevertheless Krug persisted in his efforts to sway Nietzsche, even sending him the copy which he had made himself of the prelude to *Tristan*. It was clear that he planned to acquire the whole score for himself when he could afford it, but meanwhile he attempted to interest the "Germania" in this project. Nietzsche, when approached with this suggestion, apparently demonstrated more eagerness to purchase Schumann's oratorio *Das Paradies und die Peri*, for in his letter of November 1861[7] Krug again found it necessary to urge the case for *Tristan* in a comparison of the two works:

> So schön und vollendet es [Schumann's oratorio] auch ist, fehlt doch oft das Eigenthümliche, wonach Du strebst, und ich glaube an Tristan und Isolde könnten wir noch mehr haben, indem wir, als an einem tieferen Werke, daran länger studiren könnten, um es vollständig zu be-

greifen und zu erfassen. Jedenfalls wollen wir uns die wichtige Berathung, ob wir uns das letztere anschaffen wollen, bis Weihnachten aufsparen, da man über diesem wichtigen Gegenstand keinen voreiligen Entschluß fassen darf. (HKB I, 387)

Krug's efforts at winning Nietzsche's support in this matter must have failed, otherwise he would not have found it necessary to act on his own in April 1862, not only transgressing the regulations of the club but also precipitating the financial crisis alluded to above. Meanwhile his contributions to the "Germania" underscore his steady interest in the phenomenon Wagner – including a report on *Das Rheingold* to the synod meeting of March 1862. In this instance it was clear that he was not giving his "colleagues" the benefit of his independent study of the work in question (the preview copy arrived on April 1, according to his own report [HK II, 443]): Krug had other sources at his disposal, including a musical weekly such as the *Neue Zeitschrift für Musik*, founded by Robert Schumann to champion new music, and subsequently edited by the Wagnerian Franz Brendel. Other than Elisabeth's assertion (*Leben* I, 135) there is no evidence whatever that the "Germania" subscribed to this paper in one of its first official acts or even later. It was too specialized a periodical for the limited budget of the club, and since it was consistently Krug who passed on information gleaned from it in his letters, it is likely that it was the subscription of the elder Krug which was being so exploited. A more logical choice for the "Germania" was indeed Brendel's newer periodical, the *Anregungen für Kunst, Leben und Wissenschaft*, which the members definitely considered in the summer of 1861 (HKB I, 376). Editor Franz Brendel, whom Nietzsche later remembered in his *Ecce homo* as the Wagnerian who confused Wagner with Hegel (XV, 75), envisioned it as a forum which should bring together all of the arts, philosophy and the sciences. Since its inception he had reserved his more theoretical and frankly Wagnerian utterances for it rather than for the *Neue Zeitschrift für Musik*. The volume for 1856, which was ultimately made available to the club, contained no less than six essays on Wagner and related matters by Brendel alone, and others by Richard Pohl and Arnold Schloenbach. Arthur Schopenhauer was also discussed in its pages, although there is no indication that Nietzsche took note of the fact. By 1861 the magazine was already moribund, but its back issues literally formed the library of Wagnerian theory for the club. Brendel is the highest authority ever quoted in Wagnerian matters by the members of the "Germania" in the extant documents (HK II, 441).

For the time being all discussion about words and music and their relationship in the new art form seemed to have been pre-empted by members Krug and Pinder, while Nietzsche was typically concerned with something more basic, as revealed in his proposed topic for a prize essay: "Über das

Wesen der Musik" (HK II, 94). Unfortunately nothing of this undertaking has come down to us other than a few notes and jottings made by Nietzsche in formulating the problem and experimenting with the rhetoric he would use in his arguments. In these he contrasts in vivid metaphor the radical extremes of music known to him, the dry-as-dust fugues of Albrechtsberger and the passionate tides of the *Tristan* music, and finds that neither intellectual nor emotional elements can be essential to the musical experience (HK II, 114), but rather "der ursprüngliche Eindruck dämonischer Natur" (HK II, 89).[8]

> Daß dies Dämonische von den Hörern nachempfunden wird, ist also das höchste Erforderniß zum Kunstverständniß. Das ist aber weder ein Gefühl noch ein Erkennen, sondern ein dumpfes Ahnen des Göttlichen. Durch Bewegung entsteht dies Gefühl, wo aus der Form plötzlich der Himmelsfunke herausschlägt; symbolisch ist es Bewegung des Kosmos. (HK II, 172)

There is nothing here that would betray a familiarity with Wagner's basic conception of music in *Oper und Drama* as the *means* for the expression of a dramatic idea definable apart from music. Rather than any sympathy with the Feuerbachian sensationalism that colors much of Wagnerian theory,[9] the fragmentary remains of the essay "Über das Wesen der Musik" reveal an early kinship in Nietzsche's speculation with the music metaphysics of Schopenhauer. Music for Nietzsche was already a symbolism paralleling the fundamental motions of the universe.

It would however be a mistake to assume that the discussions of music and drama which took place in the "Germania" were entirely without echo in Nietzsche's own thinking; they may well account for the particular turn taken in his school essay on *Oedipus rex* of 1864. Here his peripheral speculations on the function of music in the choruses of Aeschylus and Sophocles lent themselves to a direct comparison with "das was die neuste musikalische Schule als das Ideal des 'Kunstwerks der Zukunft' aufstellt, Werke in denen die edelsten Künste sich zu einer harmonischen Vereinigung zusammenfinden" (HK II, 376-377). But as the further discussion in this essay demonstrates, no more than the most superficial grasp of Wagnerian theory, we may conclude that Nietzsche had in the meantime made no effort to acquaint himself with Wagner's ideas at first hand. For the student of Nietzsche's development it is worth noting that the central dichotomy of *Die Geburt der Tragödie* is already germinally present in these early essays, antedating his acquaintance with Schopenhauer's philosophy as well as his closer association with Wagner. The step from the Demonic to the Dionysian nature of music was but a further refinement in terminology, and in Nietzsche's careful attention to elements of lyrical form, symmetry and restraint in the *Oedipus* commentary the

Apollonian deity was present in spirit, if not yet in name.[10]

When in 1864 Nietzsche reviewed the benefits accruing to him from the activities of the "Germania," he showed no appreciation of the broadening of his musical horizon to include *Tristan und Isolde* and the music-dramatic theories of its composer; rather his gratitude was reserved for the standards of literary and musical production to which he felt compelled by the participation in this regulated critical forum. We are clearly indebted to the "Germania" for some early essays which would scarcely have been well received by his teachers at Pforta, notably "Fatum und Geschichte" and "Willensfreiheit und Fatum," which in their anticipation of motifs of Nietzsche's later writings reveal a continuity of thought for which this philosopher is not popularly noted.[11] Nietzsche was particularly thankful that the platform afforded his musical compositions by the "Germania" had provoked him "durch ein gründliches Erlernen der Compositionslehre" (HK III, 68) to counter the ill effects of his habit of free improvisation at the piano.

II. MUSIC AND THE CREATIVE IMPULSE

Under the critical auspices of the "Germania" Gustav Krug had further opportunity to influence his friend musically, and the evidence shows that he was not hesitant in pointing out the deficiencies in Nietzsche's control of the craft of musical composition and in prompting him to greater clarity and logic (HK II, 442). The admonitions of Krug did not go unheeded. Just how exhaustive Nietzsche's renewed struggle with the intricacies of theory and composition may have been is a matter for debate, but the indications are that he now turned to the works of the noted contrapuntist J. G. Albrechtsberger, which had been republished by Seyfried as late as 1837 in an edition designed "zum Selbstunterricht."[12] A decade later Nietzsche wrote in the draft of a letter to Hans von Bülow: "[Ich] besitze die Theorie durch Studium Albrechtberger's [sic], habe Fugen *en masse* geschrieben und bin des reinen Stils – bis zu einem gewissen Grad der Reinheit fähig" (HKB III, 308).

Of the "Fugen *en masse*" not a great number have "survived," if that is the proper term, but of the compositions or sketches which still exist there is a very noticeable concentration of contrapuntally oriented works dating from the years 1860 and 1861. The available manuscript scores have a neat, workmanlike appearance – due as much to the clear, pen-and-ink notation of the composer as to his persistence in what appears at first glance to be a strict contrapuntal style whose archaic aspect is enhanced by the abundance of breves, whole- and half-note values. Typical of Nietzsche's attempts at strict or "pure" style is the "Miserere" dating from the summer of 1860. This piece and other polyphonic studies of the immediate period show the composer's effort to conform to the principles of the older vocal counterpoint deriving from Palestrina and long nurtured in the musical academies. There is a general avoidance of chromatic lines and clear modulation. The chief defect beyond a certain awkwardness is the lack of any real harmonic definition or melodic continuity despite the recurring motifs. Here as later Nietzsche found it inconvenient to force his ideas into the rigid fugal mold with its clear-cut tonic-dominant key relationships; his fugal "expositions" show the subjects and countersubjects entering in succession, but the usual cycle of keys is rarely followed,[13] and his pieces are quite likely to end in an unexpected and unexplainable tonality. Both the voice-leading and the notation itself suggest composition at the keyboard; Nietzsche frequently omitted all key signatures and then forgot to add the appropriate accidentals in the process of recording the notes.

It is perfectly consistent with this actively contrapuntal phase in Nietzsche's musical creativity that the oratorio attracted him very much at this time. Spurred on by the "Germania," he set about composing a Christmas Oratorio, of which a series of studies, fragments, and completed numbers are extant; these span the period from the summer of 1860 to that of 1861. Most of these items were dated by Nietzsche himself, so that it is possible to relate them chronologically to the

Easter recess of 1861, when he and Krug first played through sections of the new score of *Tristan und Isolde*. Throughout this period Nietzsche exhibited an unabating predilection for contrapuntal techniques, to the point where Krug felt obliged to caution him against the inclusion of too many extended fugues in his oratorio, "da dies leicht ermüdet und oft einen trockenen Eindruck macht" (HKB I, 369). Despite his enthusiasm for fugue-writing Nietzsche's scores show that he invariably ran into difficulties with this form: after brave beginnings his fugues soon degenerate into simpler textures, and there are numerous violations of the canons of part-writing without compelling reason. Although Nietzsche's mastery of this idiom does not significantly increase during this period, there is a noticeable shift in the underlying harmonic basis of his writing. It appears very much as if Wagner's masterpiece of free-flowing chromatic counterpoint had provided him with the impetus for new experiments in polyphony and harmony, a foreshadowing of the role *Tristan* was to play generally in the development of modern music. As late as March 1861 Nietzsche was still holding the line against the intrusion of harmonic novelties – and this despite the dominance of the harmonic element in his musical imagination. The "Einleitung und Chor" (August 1860) from his oratorio is in a strictly traditional, although well-developed harmonic idiom: its opening might have been inspired by the B-flat minor prelude from Book I of the *Well-Tempered Clavier*. Likewise the "Einleitung zur Verkündigung Mariae," which bears the critical date: March 1861. But the "Mariensverkündigung mit Fuge," begun as early as February and completed in May 1861, shows a curious mixture of styles. Most significantly the fugue, perhaps Nietzsche's longest and most consistently executed work in this form (93 bars), employs chromatics freely although its main subject is completely diatonic. Toward the close especially there are striking passages colored by chromatically sagging harmonies in the Wagnerian vein. Although the piece concludes abruptly in B major, the tonal center is more accurately described as A minor or F major; but in all fairness, this kind of tonal anarchy cannot be ascribed to Wagner's influence.

Ordinarily it might be risky, if not foolish, to claim that Nietzsche let himself be consciously influenced by Wagner while working on his oratorio; certainly the few parallels hitherto noted would be inconclusive evidence. But in the "Hirtenchor und Gesang des Mohren" and the following "Sternerwartung," begun during Easter vacation (HK I, 247) and showing the date June 1861, the signs are clearer. In the opaque, alliterative text given to the Moor Nietzsche included an unmistakable token of the proximity of *Tristan und Isolde:* "Wild wogt der Wahn, wo durch bewegt, das Wunder wollend mein Gemüth? [*sic*]" Equally unambiguous is the Wagnerian musical imprint. The "Hirtenchor" proves to be a chromatic canon in four voices, and the "Sternerwartung" section little more than an improvisatory exercise in Wagnerian chromatic suspensions. Mention must also be made of a short number which Nietzsche considered for the end of the oratorio but to which Krug objected because of its excessively lugubrious nature (HKB I, 369). "Der Könige Tod" is likewise an experiment in slow, persistently sagging chromatic progressions, and here the composer so creatively absorbed the idiosyncrasies of Wagner that he was surprised in later years to note how closely he had approached the sonorities of *Parsifal* (GB IV, 110-111).

Perhaps the most radical excursion in musical eccentricity which Nietzsche ever undertook is his "Schmerz ist der Grundton der Natur," presented to the "Germania" in August 1861. In the available manuscript this is a fragmentary work scored for piano duet. It begins ambitiously as a fugue with two subjects; however the counterpoint soon deteriorates, and the mournful if not unbearable aspect of nature is expressed in an abundance of acrid dissonances and generally chaotic part-writing. This is a purely experimental piece (possibly even a satire?), and it illustrates Nietzsche's typical habit of exploring an idea or a technique to its ultimate implications. As music this work must be termed a total failure; it is more successful as a demonstration of what misdeeds were possible in composition after Wagner had effectively undermined the traditional concepts of form and of harmonic continuity. Such appears to have been the work's function for Nietzsche. It might even be said that Wagner represented a new problem in terms of musical language which Nietzsche had pursued to its virtual limits before rejecting it as insoluble. For he could go no further in this direction.

It appears incontestable that, for a few months at least, Nietzsche's own musical language underwent a characteristic change after his brief exposure to the advanced Wagnerian idiom of *Tristan*. But Wagner's extensive theories were of slight concern to him as yet, and the exchanges with Gustav Krug surely indicate that he was by no means ready to accept the work in question on the same basis as the friend who saw in it the "Culminationspunkt der Oper." But the expressive possibilities of this music – "die leidenschaftlichen Wogen Tristan und Isoldes" (HK II, 114) – had not escaped Nietzsche as a harmonic experimenter. Much as Handelian music had once inspired him to "make something similar" (HK I, 18), the impact of certain elements of Wagner's radical style was such as to require immediate verification in practice. The essential difference would lie in the fact that Nietzsche was not merely imitating Wagner (which would be remarkable in itself, if one considers the short contact with a work deemed unperformable by professional musicians of the day) but rather conducting his own experiments with the advanced harmonies shown to him fully developed in *Tristan*. As a talented dilettante he was probably more accessible to this kind of influence than a more thoroughly trained musician might have been. He did not, it should be noted, in any way abandon his attempts at writing in an anachronistic polyphonic idiom, but attempted to fuse the new idiom with the archaic forms of the oratorio. That Nietzsche should have chanced upon some Parsifalesque sonorities twenty years before Wagner completed his "Bühnenweihfestspiel," is only a demonstration that he was concerned not with the particular result achieved by Wagner, but with the exploration of his techniques. In 1882 Nietzsche preferred to interpret the coincidence as proof of the cultural decadence which he had shared with Wagner even as a young man, but as a matter of record, Nietzsche's "vitality" in this early period was reaffirmed in his marked retreat from the extremes of these early compositions, a tendency already noticeable in the symphonic poem "Ermanarich" begun in September 1861, revised and completed a year later.

The theme of the great Gothic hero was of more than passing interest to Nietzsche, as is shown in the variety of media in which it aroused him creatively. There was a lecture to the "Germania" in July 1861, subsequently a poem, "Ermanarichs Tod," an opera scenario, and later a series of school essays on the various saga traditions, in addition to the tone poem itself. In this composition Nietzsche was still attempting to translate his conception of somber grandeur directly into musical terms and was hence not above grasping at crudely unconventional means. But the eccentricities are isolated, and the insistent rhythmic pulse and the long sections of clearly definable tonality are more significant in the character of the whole than the musical neologisms. Nietzsche left a detailed "program" for this work, which only underlines the disparity between poetic intention and musical realization. When he wrote this commentary on the work a year later, even the composer had grown critical of the extremes of his musical language:

> Der Weltschmerz wird durch seltsame Harmonien eingeführt, die sehr herbe und schmerzlich sind und mir anfangs durchaus mißfielen. Jetzt erscheinen sie mir durch den Gang des Ganzen etwas wenigstens gemildert und entschuldigt. Das Drängen und Jagen der Leidenschaft zuletzt mit ihren plötzlichen Übergängen und stürmischen Ausbrüchen strotzt von harmonischen Ungeheuerlichkeiten, über die ich nicht zu entscheiden wage. (HK II, 104)

The parallel between this piece and Wagner's glorification of myth readily comes to mind, but Nietzsche nowhere suggests that Wagner's theory or example played a role in its conception. Rather it was one of the national tone poems of Liszt which he had taken as his model: "...ich [hatte] den Plan... ähnlich wie in der "Hungaria" Liszt's geschehen, die Gefühlswelt eines slavischen Volkes in einer Composition zu umfassen" (HK II, 101). For a time he had considered entitling the piece simply "Serbia."

Two further larger instrumental works dating from the following year (1863) show a continuation of the tendency toward "purification" of Nietzsche's musical language. Although the first of these, a "Große Sonate" for pianoforte, remained a fragment, the formal implications of the genre itself and the total absence of lugubrious chromatics of the Wagnerian type are indicative of the trend. Also its rhythmic vigor and the stormy vitality of its crashing chords and passage-work set it apart from those compositions directly under the *Tristan* spell. Even "Eine Sylvesternacht" (for violin and piano), despite its pretentions as program music, shows further refinement in the same "undecadent" direction of simpler textures, less overwrought straining for expression, and greater tonal coherency. But this piece is the last large-scale instrumental work belonging to the period prior to Nietzsche's meeting with Wagner, actually before 1871. In the meanwhile, and even before these compositions, Nietzsche had been increasingly turning to the smaller instrumental and vocal forms.

Nietzsche's mazurkas, csárdáses, and Hungarian marches have apparently not survived to any extent the recent relocation of the old Nietzsche Archive, but most of the Lieder had already been published in a single volume in 1924.[14] Krug's comment on the new pieces Nietzsche submitted to the "Germania" in February 1862 ("Ungarische Skizzen") are indicative of the new trend, which was not unwelcome even to the original Wagner enthusiast of the club: "Der Componist zeigte darin einen viel geläuteteren [sic] Sinn, als in seinen früheren Werken, Schumann'scher Einfluss ist nicht zu verkennen, jedoch fällt der Componist niemals in Nachahmung" (HK II, 442). Nietzsche's Lieder, written between 1862 and 1865, are available to those who would take the trouble to locate the published scores and need not be treated in any detail here. They may, in the words of the somewhat impatient Ernest Newman, exhibit "the rankest amateurism" (Newman IV, 323), but they also reveal in their unpretentiousness and restraint that Nietzsche was potentially capable of creating small-scale works of art with genuine musical feeling and continuity, something which his earlier "monstrosities" do not suggest. There is nothing whatever Wagnerian about these works; they use to good advantage the harmonies familiar to the lovers of Schumann and Brahms, conjure up moods of nostalgia and gentle melancholy appropriate to their texts by Klaus Groth, Rückert, Petöfi and Pushkin. In all likelihood these Lieder were composed at the piano too – the melodies are conceived more in terms of the keyboard than the voice – and the musical orthography and patterns of tonality now and then leave something to be desired, but they do encompass Nietzsche's most successful compositions, even a few worthy of occasional performance.

If further evidence be required of Nietzsche's basically unshaken musical preferences in the period after his introduction to *Tristan*, it may be found in the hints as to his daily musical consumption at Schulpforta contained in the requests for music sent to his mother and sister. These include music by Haydn, Mozart and Beethoven, Schubert and in particular Schumann. Toward the end of his study at Schulpforta Nietzsche developed a mild curiosity about the music of Liszt, apparently unrelated to his earlier exposures through the "Germania," and involving mainly the *Consolations* for piano (HK II, 406) and the *Faustsymphonie*. However there is no sign of outspoken enthusiasm here (*cf*. HKB I, 253).

As a student in Bonn the following year Nietzsche was active in attending concerts, and he even participated in the mammoth chorus of the Lower Rhenish Music Festival of 1865; but we never hear him complain that these events almost exclusively favored the classical repertory and the proven conservatives among the contemporary composers. The single hint of Nietzsche's reaction to this state of affairs may be seen in a wilfully avant-garde setting of one of his less worthy poems ("Junge Fischerin") for voice and piano. But even "Junge Fischerin" is notably free from experimental harmonies, although it represents in other aspects an extravagant departure from the strophic simplicity of his "serious" Lieder. An amused description of this latest experiment in a letter to his sister may best restrain us from overestimating its importance: "Es ist ein Lied im höchsten Zukunftsstile mit einem natürlichen Aufschrei und dergleichen Ingredienzen [*sic*] einer stillen Narrheit" (HKB I, 331-332).

Perhaps Nietzsche's attitude toward Wagner and the moderns during this early period may best be characterized as a playful eclecticism. His imitations of "modern" eccentricities did not in any way constitute a serious attempt to forge a coherent musical language of his own. His most active concern with the Wagnerian idiom coincided in time with a marked reserve in his overall enthusiasm for Wagner's work – as contrasted with Gustav Krug's missionary fervor – and the sporadic indulgences in "futuristic" techniques in the later phase were at best tongue-in-cheek obeisances to the powers that would soon dominate the musical scene. His true sympathies clearly lay elsewhere, although he never completely turned his back on the moderns.

III. THE AESTHETIC PROBLEM OF THE NEW MUSIC

When Nietzsche transferred to Leipzig at the end of his first year of university study, he did so, according to the implication of one of his autobiographical accounts, in order to follow his professor, Friedrich Ritschl (HK V, 255). But he admitted at the time that the lure of Leipzig was also a musical one. He had every intention of pursuing the study of music in a way not possible in Bonn, and particularly of developing his critical acumen through historical studies and increased exposure to recent works (HKB I, 333). In the recesses of his mind lurked the possibility of abandoning classical philology altogether in favor of music; it was surely his plan of self-education rather than any abrupt turn from the conservative interests most manifest in the recent past which accounted for his new eagerness in Leipzig to expose himself to the music of the moderns. Certainly Nietzsche's reading lists from the Bonn period give no indication of any further exploration of modernist theory; these suggest that he was concerned with historical aspects of western music. Specifically mentioned are authors Karl Fortlage, noted for his studies of the music of ancient Greece, August Reissmann, author of a conservative history of music and a new monograph on Schumann, and the rather dated *Beethoven* of Adolf Bernhard Marx (HK III, 99).[15] Nietzsche's reading was not, however, restricted to historical works, and the inclusion of a single name in his reading list for the Easter vacation of 1865 shows that the old concern with basic aesthetic problems of music was still alive: Eduard Hanslick. When Nietzsche's library was catalogued in 1942,[16] it still contained a well-marked copy of the 1865 edition of Hanslick's sobering little polemic, *Vom Musikalisch-Schönen*. In Nietzsche's notes of the same year there is a clear parallel to Hanslick's view of the natural limitations of music as an expressive medium.[17]

As a result of the enormously effective barrage of invective aimed at him from Bayreuth, the brilliant Viennese critic Hanslick is known to the music public today almost exclusively in the image painted of him by his enemies. He lives on in the figure of a rule-bound Beckmesser obstructing the advance of true musical art. Yet in a century which was passionately devoted to the unlimited expansion of the possibilities of musical representation and in which increasingly fanciful literary interpretations of the abstract music of the Viennese classicists were the order of the day, Hanslick achieved prominence as one of the few articulate voices of reason and moderation. For him the "content" of music could only be music itself ("tönend bewegte Formen"), never a poetic or dramatic "program." While Liszt, Berlioz and Wagner were completing the process of disintegration of the formal principles of classical music and even their lesser contemporaries were more dependent on the guidance of the literary word in their music than any composers since the early operatic monodists, it was understandable that Hanslick became the spokesman for musical conservatives like Brahms who still found it possible to develop within the framework of traditional formal principles and to write self-contained musical structures independent of poetic program or plot.

Very possibly it was Nietzsche's association with Hermann Deiters in Bonn, the future author of the first authoritative biography of Brahms,[18] which led him in 1865 to Hanslick's book, originally published a decade earlier. Although the aesthetic problem was not new to Nietzsche, the overwhelming preponderance of strophic Lieder among his recent compositions – in the wake of harmonically and structurally ambiguous experiments – suggests that he was ripe for the formalistic theory of Hanslick. Indeed his growing critical awareness early in 1865 led him to abjure further composition altogether (HK III, 118; HKB II, 333), a resolution which accounts for the abrupt decline in his musical output during the next years. At the University of Bonn Nietzsche had before him in Otto Jahn the example of a classical philologist who had successfully applied his professional acumen to the problem of Mozart's biography,[19] and it is surely no coincidence that Jahn's name and "Meine Absichten als Recensent und Musikhistoriker" are juxtaposed in the notes reviewing his year at Bonn (HK III, 118). At a point of indecision between philology and music Nietzsche was, in short, attempting to provide himself with a solid basis in music history and aesthetics, but his studies of 1865 all have a clear conservative bias.

It is the latter which stands out in his encounter with the new piano score of *Die Walküre* in the spring of 1866. Despite his gesture of historical impartiality in the fragmentary "review" which has been preserved, he betrays the hostility of a Hanslick toward "dramatic" music which does not conform to the demands of purely musical interest and continuity. In what may have been a "practice" critique of the work, Nietzsche begins with a rhetorical stress on the aesthetic problem itself: can a new Lessing be found who will pace off the limits of music as opposed to poetry? The reviewer is at pains to demonstrate the temporary character of any judgment on the phenomenon Wagner before the end of his creative span had been reached. In discussing the actual music however, about which he expresses mixed feeling elsewhere (HKB II, 97-98), Nietzsche gets very little further than the orchestral introduction. The ironic commentary here is characteristic:

> Wüßten wir nicht, daß Sturm gemalt werden soll, so würden wir rathen zunächst auf ein wirbelndes Rad, dann auf einen vorbeibrausenden Dampfzug. Wir hören das Klappern der Räder, den einförmigen Rythmus, das pausenlose dahinjagende Getöse. Es wird uns bei längerem Anhören schwindelnd.... (HK III,208)

Whether Nietzsche's critical attitude might have been softened by the experience of an orchestral performance remains conjectural; at best he could have heard this music in the series of ten "Zukunftsmatineen" announced for the winter of 1865-66 in Leipzig (*cf.* HKB II, 404-405). Yet the indications in the *Neue Zeitschrift für Musik* are that not more than four of these matinees were actually held,[20] and that much more conventional music supplanted the ambitiously avant-garde programs originally scheduled. Some few Lieder of Wagner and Liszt were ultimately performed in the series, the closing scene from *Tristan*, and a four-hand version of Liszt's tone poem *Mazeppa;* but Nietzsche himself mentions the "Zukunftsmatineen" only once after his initial enthusiastic references to the forthcoming concerts in letters home (HKB II, 20, 22; *cf.* HK III, 313). As an alert young man in a musically active city he wanted to keep abreast of new developments, but the depth of his sympathies with the modernists is apparent both in a comment to Gersdorff dating from his second semester in Leipzig – "Drei Dinge sind meine Erholungen, aber seltene Erholungen, mein Schopenhauer, Schumannsche Musik, endlich einsame Spaziergänge" (HKB II, 45) – and in a list of "musikalische mignonnes" made after his fourth semester. Represented here prominently are works by Schumann, Beethoven, and Schubert. Two choral works of Bach are mentioned, "ein paar" Lieder of Brahms, and of Wagner only the early opera *Tannhäuser*, listed indiscriminately next to a work by Meyerbeer (HK III, 316). It is highly indicative of his tastes, at least up to the beginning of his tour of duty as a cavalry officer, that Nietzsche was attracted to works firmly in the grand opera tradition, including the most "advanced" work of Wagner over which Eduard Hanslick could still wax at all enthusiastic. Nietzsche had at least the opportunity to hear music from *Tristan* performed orchestrally in Leipzig,[21] but if he attended the concert in question there is no indication of his reaction to it. Despite all outward open-mindedness there are no real signs of a weakening in his fundamentally conservative attitude until the spring and summer of 1868, only a few months before his personal encounter with Wagner.

IV. MUSIC AND METAPHYSICS

It is inevitable that the name of Schopenhauer should enter the pages of our portrayal, for the musical philosopher appears to loom significantly on the road from Nietzsche's conservatism to his ultimate conversion to the "music of the future." Certainly some evaluation of the role played by the philosophy of Will in hastening – or perhaps hindering – this development is in order. From the time of Nietzsche's "fateful" encounter with *Die Welt als Wille und Vorstellung* in Rohn's bookstore during his first weeks in Leipzig to his public reaffirmation of faith nine years later in *Schopenhauer als Erzieher*, the frequency of allusion to "Schopenhauer *und* Wagner" raises the question of their relative function. It is with this question in mind that we look again at the record.

There is no doubt that some of the immediate appeal of the writings of this "gloomy genius" (HK III, 298) was conditioned by the uncommonly pessimistic mood in which Nietzsche found himself on arrival in Leipzig. There, cut off from old friends, both relieved and depressed over his forceful severance from the wastrel fraternal life of the "Franconia," he was still in doubt as to his future profession and troubled by more intangible matters as well. Although he had ultimately prevailed over his family in rejecting theology as his field of study, the attendant metaphysical questions were to remain with him. Schopenhauer's writings seemed made for such a phase in the development of a young iconoclast. Impressive as a stylist among philosophers, Schopenhauer inspired awe as a writer steeped in the literary culture of antiquity and in the science of his own day; moreover he was fearless in his search for truth and just as relentless in proclaiming it – often to the discomfiture of his enemies. Most importantly, Schopenhauer's denial of any underlying rational basis in nature, a radical departure from the mainstream of European metaphysics, tended to justify and stimulate Nietzsche's thinking along similar lines. That Schopenhauer conceived of the aesthetic experience as one of the central avenues of escape from the insistent demands of the irrational Will clearly endeared him to Nietzsche. A letter written home as early as November 5, 1865 further witnesses to the impact made by Schopenhauer's praise of the ascetic life as the means for permanently negating the Will (HKB II, 19), as does Nietzsche's own abortive attempt to deny the flesh through deliberate rejection of necessary sleep:

> Auch leibliche Peinigungen fehlten nicht. So zwang ich mich 14 Tage hintereinander immer erst um 2 Uhr Nachts zu Bett zu gehen und es genau um 6 Uhr wieder zu verlassen. Eine nervöse Aufgeregtheit bemächtigte sich meiner. ... (HK III, 298)

For his pious mother he was still able to interpret Schopenhauer within the framework of early Christianity (cf. HKB II, 19), since the philosopher, despite his denial of any moral substratum in the universe, still preached a basically Christian ethic of asceticism and compassion. In Michael Landmann's view it was precisely in Nietzsche's *joyful* affirmation of the amoral substratum that he ultimately parted company with Schopenhauer. "Da es für Nietzsche keine Legitimation mehr giebt, von der aus wir das Unlogische und Wertindifferente der Weltordnung betrauern können, bleibt uns nichts übrig als es hinzunehmen und uns dazu zu bekennen."[22] Actually the critical divergence from his teacher which would eventually lead to his conception of the Dionysian was apparent in his inversion of Schopenhauerian terms in a letter to Gersdorff as early as April 8, 1866:

> Gestern stand ein stattliches Gewitter am Himmel, ich eilte auf einen benachbarten Berg. ... Das Gewitter entlud sich höchst gewaltig mit Sturm und Hagel, ich empfand einen unvergleichlichen Aufschwung und ich erkannte recht, wie wir erst dann die Natur recht verstehen, wenn wir zu ihr aus unsern Sorgen und Bedrängnissen heraus flüchten müßen. Was war mir der Mensch und sein unruhiges Wollen! Was war mir das ewige "Du sollst" "Du sollst nicht"! Wie anders der Blitz, der Sturm, der Hagel, freie Mächte, ohne Ethik! Wie glücklich, wie kräftig sind sie, reiner Wille, ohne Trübungen durch den Intellekt! (HKB II, 45)

Could there be a more telling displacement of the greatest good preached by Schopenhauer: the deemphasis of the Will realized in the Genius, the

Saint, and in the fleeting moment of aesthetic contemplation? Of the ideal which he might have designated "reiner Intellekt, ohne Trübungen durch den Willen"?

Even such a basic difference of sympathy as is apparent in this single spontaneous exclamation, seemed in no way to affect Nietzsche's enthusiasm for the philosophy of pessimism, which he soon communicated to his friends. With Gersdorff and Mushacke he carried on lively readings and discussions (HKB II, 32). Soon a new friend joined the group in Leipzig, the philology student Erwin Rohde, probably the most gifted member of Nietzsche's immediate circle. In these years he directed many another to the works of Schopenhauer and rejoiced whenever he could register a "conversion." Thus it was with his schoolmate Paul Deussen, who was studying theology in Tübingen. Although Deussen held out more stubbornly than any of Nietzsche's closer friends, he in time became the most devoted Schopenhauer disciple of all. And it was not much different with Pastor F. A. Wenkel of Naumburg, of whom Nietzsche wrote in June 1868 to Rohde:

> Auch er hat jetzt das Bild Schopenhauers in seiner Studirstube aufgehängt. Seine Gespräche haben gar kein anderes und lieberes Objekt als ethische Probleme; wärst Du in Naumburg, so hättest Du das Vergnügen Schopenhauer von der Kanzel herab zu hören. Was mir noch besonders werth ist: Wenkel hat einen mäch-

tigen Respekt vor der Persönlichkeit, auch vor der moralischen Sch.'s. (HKB II, 213)

Nietzsche himself was at least as much impressed by the literary personality of his philosopher as by any idea or set of ideas expounded by him. Here was an image of singular nobility in an age which glorified mediocrity, a welcome antidote to the mid-nineteenth century cult of optimism and progress.

From the beginning of his interest Nietzsche had not shielded himself from the critics of his idol (such as Rudolf Haym and Friedrich Ueberweg) and was by no means immune to the problems lying at the root of Schopenhauer's thought. In the spirit of F. A. Lange's *Geschichte des Materialismus*, which he read in the summer of 1866, Nietzsche demonstrated the basic epistemological difficulty of any statement about the *Ding an sich* (such as that equating it with Will), and then went on to develop a practical apologia for his interest in a philosopher like Schopenhauer. Proceeding from the Kantian skepticism regarding the nature of ultimate reality, Lange had advocated the tolerance of all metaphysics, including that implied in materialist systems, on a more or less pragmatic basis. Any particular interpretation of ultimate reality was accordingly open to question as "truth," but at least might have substantial validity on an aesthetic or devotional plane, even if it could not form the working basis for experimental science.

> Folglich, meint Lange, lasse man die Philosophen frei, vorausgesetzt, daß sie uns hinfüro erbauen. Die Kunst ist frei, auch auf dem Gebiet der Begriffe. Wer will einen Satz von Beethoven widerlegen...? Du siehst, selbst bei diesem strengsten kritischen Standpunkte bleibt uns unser Schopenhauer, ja er wird uns fast noch mehr. Wenn die Philosophie Kunst ist, dann mag auch Haym sich vor Schopenhauer verkriechen; wenn die Philosophie erbauen soll, dann kenne ich wenigstens keinen Philosophen, der mehr erbaut als unser Schopenhauer. (HKB II, 83)

On the reluctant Paul Deussen Nietzsche consequently did not try to impress the virtues of Schopenhauer through logical discourse, nor did he attempt to counter the individual objections voiced by this friend. Nietzsche's rejoinder amounted rather to a confession of faith, the conscious rejection of logic by the religious intellectual.

> Wer mir Schopenhauer durch Gründe widerlegen will, dem raune ich ins Ohr: "Aber lieber Mann, Weltanschauungen werden weder durch Logik geschaffen, noch vernichtet. Ich fühle mich heimisch in jenem Dunstkreis, Du in jenem. ..." Wenn ein Sklave im Gefängniß träumt, er sei frei und entbunden seiner Knechtschaft, wer wird so hartherzig sein, ihn zu wecken und ihm zu sagen, daß es ein Traum sei? (HKB II, 154)

If such passages tend to illuminate the metaphysical need which was filled for Nietzsche by Schopenhauer's philosophy, they also suggest the instability of this fulfillment in the very awareness of a distinction between belief and better judgment. In later years Nietzsche stigmatized this kind of escapism in a more violent formula: "Credo quia absurdum est."

By the time of his tour of military training in the winter of 1867-68 there were indications that the intensity of the Schopenhauer phase had begun to taper off. These took variously the forms of humorous self-ironization, nostalgic recollection of his earlier uncomplicated enthusiasm, and increased analytical attention to the logical difficulties in Schopenhauer's "system." A certain increased perspective if not actual distance, for example, was reflected in the growing tendency to jest about his "addiction" to Schopenhauer, as may be noted in Nietzsche's amused account to Rohde of his incongruous appeals to this deity ("Schopenhauer hilf") while "unter dem Bauch des Pferdes versteckt" (HKB II, 158), or in a typically self-conscious remark on the influence of Schopenhauer: "... mir ist es so, als ob Du bei den niedergeschriebenen Zeilen den Duft von Schopenhauerischer Küche riechen müßtest" (HKB II, 174). As late as June 1868 Nietzsche was still able to rejoice over a new "conversion" to Schopenhauer, but he did so with an envious consciousness of his own remoteness from the experience of the convert:

> Ich... erlebe in der Begeisterungsflamme dieses Mannes von neuem den ersten Rausch der "jungen Liebe," jene Leipziger Herbsttage, in denen zum ersten Male jene wundersame Schopenhauersche Musik mir das Herz im tiefsten löste. (HKB II, 212-213)

Most significantly, Nietzsche felt a new urge to work out in detail the improbabilities of Schopenhauer's main premises beyond the rather general skepticism in regard to metaphysics of the Lange type. During the course of his long recuperation from a troublesome injury Nietzsche undertook to elaborate the difficulties in several pages of closely reasoned argument. The central concern was, of course, with Schopenhauer's intuitive interpretation of the *Ding an sich* as Will and the logical contradictions resulting from the attempt to delineate its characteristics:

> Zudritt sind wir gezwungen uns gegen die Prädikate zu verwahren die Schopenhauer seinem Willen beilegt, welche für etwas Schlechthin-Undenkbares viel zu bestimmt lauten und durchweg aus dem Gegensatze zur Vorstellungswelt gewonnen sind: während zwischen dem Ding an sich und der Erscheinung nicht einmal der Begriff des Gegensatzes eine Bedeutung hat. (HK III, 354)

While conceding the possibility that Schopenhauer had been correct in his intuition, Nietzsche saw clearly that the compounding of possibility in the several steps toward a delineation of Will as a meaningful concept (he spoke in terms of "eine dreifache potenzierte Möglichkeit") effectively reduced the probability of "truth" almost to the vanishing point. But even if he assumed that Schopenhauer's inspired guesswork had been correct, it was the difficulty of forcing the world into a system unified in a single metaphysical insight which disturbed Nietzsche.

> Das Schopenhauersche Grundgewebe verstrickt sich in seinen Händen: zum kleinsten Theil in Folge einer gewissen taktischen Ungeschicklichkeit seines Urhebers [,] zumeist aber weil die Welt sich nicht so bequem in das System einspannen läßt als Schopenhauer in der ersten Finderbegeisterung gehofft hatte. (HK III, 355)

If this was not an early manifestation of the suspicion of all systematic philosophy as fundamentally dishonest which distinguishes Nietzsche in the great tradition of western thought since the Renaissance, it was clearly less benign than F. A. Lange's view of metaphysics as a form of art. But Nietzsche was still far from rejecting the edifying writer and the thought-provoking genius in Schopenhauer, as is evident in aphoristic apologies found in the midst of his critique: "Die Irrthümer grosser Männer sind verehrungswürdig weil sie fruchtbarer sind als die Wahrheiten der kleinen" (HK III, 353). He insisted that he had not destroyed the usefulness of Schopenhauer's thought by exposing the weakness of his arguments or the improbability of his conclusions. For him it was a kind of esoteric poetry (Lange's term was "Begriffsdichtung") which bore the imprint of a strong personality and communicated a mood with which he was still in fundamental sympathy.

In the extant documents there is nothing as of 1868 to reflect Nietzsche's opinion of Schopenhauer's aesthetics and in particular his analysis of music. But the high rank among the arts which Schopenhauer ascribed to music was directly related to the concept of Will examined critically in Nietzsche's notes of 1868. Hence his problematic relationship to the aesthetics of Schopenhauer was implicit if not actually expressed. Looking ahead however, we note that Schopenhauer's view of music as a reflection of the Will itself in the physical world is represented prominently in *Die Geburt der Tragödie* and its preliminary stages (1870-72). In what sense, then, did Nietzsche come to terms with an idea based on a questionable metaphysical premise?

Actually the direction of his adjustment was already suggested in the notes of 1868, inasmuch as he here criticized Schopenhauer for his refusal to acknowledge "das Dunkle [,][23] Widersprechende in der Region... wo die Indiv[iduation] aufhört" (HK III, 352). Schopenhauer's transcendental Will was too clear, too shallow, too often confused with mere human will (*cf*. HK III, 357), and Nietzsche's tendency was to enrich it and deepen it in the direction of a more frankly mystical concept. In the Christian context of his school days he had seen "dämonische Kraft" (HK II, 89) as the common denominator of music and "ein dumpfes Ahnen des Göttlichen" (HK II, 172) as the listener's primary response rather than any concrete emotion or cognition, whereas by 1871 it was "das Ur-Eine," "der innerste Kern der Natur," "der geheimnisvolle Grund," "der ewige Urschmerz," "der ewige Widerspruch, der Vater der Dinge"[24] which was reflected in music, the Dionysian art. "Jene Selbstaufhebung des Willens," wrote Nietzsche in one of his plans for *Die Geburt der Tragödie*, "...ist deshalb möglich, weil der Wille nichts als Schein selbst ist, und das Ur-Eine nur in ihm eine Erscheinung hat" (IX, 178).

With the help of this momentary departure from strict chronology it can be more clearly seen that there was a continuity, if not unbroken development, in Nietzsche's thinking on aesthetics, to which Schopenhauer contributed a characteristic structure as well as a troublesome vocabulary ultimately varied by Nietzsche or charged with new meaning. In reducing the concept of Will to a position of less than central importance, Nietzsche was still able to maintain the Schopenhauerian aesthetic principle of release from the insistent demands of Will and yet to base his own metaphysics in a deeper, more positively viewed amoral substratum of empirical reality.

While Hanslick obstinately refused to go beyond music's "tönend bewegte Formen" into metaphysical speculation on the meaning of music, there was no essential conflict between his views on the autonomy of music in its highest genres and Schopenhauer's denial that music could be a representation of anything in the world of concrete phenomena. Hence it is not surprising that both writers were in agreement on the matter of the relation of words and music: words indeed require the addition of the human voice to the chorus of instruments, but as far as musical values alone are concerned, words are superfluous. It would be a mistake to think that a text can make music meaningful beyond the innate sense of music itself, although it may pleasurably engage the reflective faculties of the mind. Thus Hanslick was skeptical of the involved interpretations of the meaning of the finale of Beethoven's Ninth Symphony, while Schopenhauer went so far as to praise Rossini as the most musical of opera composers; for who else so radically ignored the sense of the texts which he set to music? In his analysis of the aesthetic experience Schopenhauer's central tenet was the disinterested contemplation of the art work by "das von den Zwecken des Willens frei gewordene, also reine Subjeckt des Erkennens"[25] – his designation for pure intellect, freed of desires and passions. Where Schopenhauer was merely descriptive Hanslick's polemic became *pre*scriptive; for he wished to counter the unmusical demands commonly made on music as a drug for the senses or a stimulant for the emotions:

> Wir setzen jenem pathologischen Ergriffenwerden das *bewußte* reine Anschauen eines Tonwerks entgegen. Diese contemplative ist die einzig künstlerische, wahre Form des Hörens; ihr gegenüber fällt der rohe Affect des Wilden und der schwärmende des Musikenthusiasten in Eine Classe. (Hanslick, 106)

With such intellectual armor[26] young Nietzsche engaged in battle with student acquaintances like Franz Hüffer in Leipzig, who was later to become one of the most influential Wagnerians in England (as critic for the London *Times*). Hüffer, who was not, like so many of Nietzsche's closer friends, temperamentally sympathetic to Schopenhauer's pessimism, was a vigorous, tactless and intellectually uncomplicated individual, as is evident both in Nietzsche's account of him and in his own subsequent lucid and uncritical popularization of Wagnerian theory, *Richard Wagner and the Music of the Future*.[27] While Hüffer responded directly to the sensuous appeal of Wagnerian music, Nietzsche remained encumbered in his approach to the ever problematic *Tristan* by intellectual and aesthetic reservations born of his love of the classical composers and nurtured by conservative writers. Nevertheless it is clear that Nietzsche had second thoughts about the extreme position he had taken when he recalled the arguments with Hüffer late in 1867:

> Ich gebe ihm [Hüffer] jetzt nachträglich zu,

daß sein musikalisches Urtheilen und Empfinden feiner, vor allem gesunder entwickelt war als das meinige. Aber damals vermochte ich dies nicht einzusehn und empfand manchen Schmerz über seinen rücksichtslosen Widerspruch. (HK III, 303-304)

V. THE MASTER SINGER

The year 1868 marks the last change of course in Nietzsche's devious approach to the art of Wagner, and not only in the sense that their personal acquaintance dates from this year. This was merely the climax of a series of incidents punctuating a gradual breakdown of Nietzsche's previous reluctance to grant Wagner his due. Externally the central event of the year was the premiere of Wagner's *Die Meistersinger* in Munich, an event which dominated the discussions in musical circles for some time. Of comparable importance was the weakening of Nietzsche's spiritual bond with Schopenhauer. Although Nietzsche continued to function as the nominal leader of a small band of Schopenhauer adherents and to communicate in the common language of this group, his earlier sympathy with the philosophy of pessimism had perceptibly cooled. Upon recovery from his military injuries Nietzsche's general mood for a long period was consistently cheerful, hopeful and even elated, as the end of his university study drew near. The contrast with his "Weltanschauungsbruder" Rohde is instructive: the latter continued to use the familiar vocabulary in a narrowly doctrinaire sense, whereas Nietzsche was increasingly disposed to express his own more dynamic attitudes as if through the mask of Schopenhauer.

Indeed the interest in Schopenhauer remained one of the basic elements of this most balanced and genuine of Nietzsche's friendships. "Der alte Oberpriester Schopenhauer schwenkt dazu den Weihkessel seiner Philosophie" (HKB II, 285), remarked Nietzsche to Rohde in concluding a grateful panegyric on the gift of such a friendship as this. For the sake of some of his more valued relationships Nietzsche undoubtedly tended to prolong the outward obeisances to Schopenhauer, but the self-conscious irony in his references to the philosopher and the increasing distortion in his use of Schopenhauer's terminology, not to mention his recent destructive analysis of Schopenhauer's metaphysics, indicate that by 1868 he had outgrown this mentor. His correspondence of the summer of that year conveys the impression that he was unusually anxious for new social and intellectual contacts, and in fact he soon proved to be more than usually susceptible to a new guiding personality.

The coincidence of the unveiling of *Die Meistersinger* with Nietzsche's period of drifting allegiance was momentous. Whereas the premiere of *Tristan und Isolde* had called forth no comment whatever in Nietzsche's correspondence or notes of 1865, it was now evident that he had made an effort to inform himself of the events in Munich through various means at his disposal. Possibly the *Neue Zeitschrift für Musik* was instrumental, which carried among other relevant items an address by Wagner to his singers and musicians, notes on the rehearsals, a review of the first performance on June 21, and finally a musical analysis of the work in seven installments by the Wagnerian Heinrich Porges. In any case Nietzsche had no reason to be embarrassed when he came face to face with the composer a few months later; this music had struck a resonance in him unmatched in any preceding Wagnerian experience.

Of all the works belonging to Wagner's mature period this single comic drama can still be counted on to win over many for whom the other operas are too slow-moving, too pretentious, too unmelodious – in short, too Wagnerian. In the age of Stravinsky and Bartók we are perhaps no longer as acutely aware of the gulf between Wagner's advanced and his conservative practice, but the quick acceptance of this masterpiece at the time shows to what degree this stylistic retrogression was appreciated by his public. Indeed it has been said that *Die Meistersinger* was Wagner's reply to those who doubted his ability to write recognizably vocal melody or respectable counterpoint. Compared with the earlier *Ring* operas and *Tristan*, which immediately preceded it in order of composition, it represents a reversion to, or relaxation in the direction of, traditionally accepted standards of harmony, tonality and musical organization; it features again the ensemble writing and the choruses of the older opera, and in its characterization of the world of the sixteenth-century artisan it is a veritable tour de force in serious and humorous mastery of the idiosyncrasies of the musical baroque – including the trills and sequences and the settings of the Protestant chorale.

Nietzsche began to familiarize himself with the music of the new work during the summer of 1868; whether or not he had procured a score during his visit to Leipzig in June is not verifiable, but it seems quite likely that he had. At the "Tonkünstlerversammlung" in Altenburg which Nietzsche attended toward the end of July no Wagnerian music was performed, but he probably heard Wagner's brother-in-law Oswald Marbach justify the new music-drama in an address "Über die Wiedergeburt der dramatischen Poesie durch Musik,"[28] which paralleled some of his own earlier thinking on the Greek drama and further stimulated him to press on his study of Wagner's music. When Rohde visited him in Naumburg in the middle of August, Nietzsche very likely played him excerpts from *Die Meistersinger*, possibly introducing him to this work; after this visit Nietzsche was able to refer to the "Meisterlied" (Prize Song) as an item definitely known to Rohde (HKB II, 265). It was the same selection that Nietzsche played to the wife of Friedrich Ritschl in Leipzig during one of his visits to their home during the summer and fall of 1868.

Ever since Bonn days Nietzsche had been on excellent terms with his professor, but the relationship had always remained rather formal. He was understandably pleased when he unexpectedly met with sympathy of a more demonstrative sort in the person of Frau Sophie Ritschl. "Frau Ritschl meine intime 'Freundin'," he wrote later in jest to Rohde (HKB II, 229). It is apparent from his letter to Sophie Ritschl of July 2 that their conversation had dealt with subjects of current interest such as Wagner and Schopenhauer, and that their discussion had not been completely harmonious. Nietzsche had played the piano for his hostess, as is suggested by his self-effacing apology for "meine Neigung zum Mißklang" (HKB II, 223), which seems at the same time to refer to his remarks on a book lent him by Frau Ritschl. Yet from the playful ambiguities of this letter it cannot be clearly established what position Nietzsche had taken in the discussions, or what music he played for the Ritschls during their June meeting. The book in question, Ludwig Ehlert's *Briefe über Musik an eine Freundin*,[29] manages to express sympathies on both sides of the Wagnerian question, and Nietzsche's comment is devoted entirely to its flamboyant style. We are nevertheless justified in assuming that his interest in Wagner's new work continued to develop during the summer, for his last resistance was gone when he reported to Rohde his attendance at the "Euterpe" concert of October 27, at which the orchestral preludes to *Tristan* and to *Die Meistersinger* were performed:

> Ich bringe es nicht übers Herz, mich dieser Musik gegenüber kritisch kühl zu verhalten; jede Faser, jeder Nerv zuckt an mir, ich habe lange nicht ein solches andauerndes Gefühl der Entrücktheit gehabt als bei letztgenannter Ouvertüre. (HKB II, 259-260)

Essentially this and similar passages in the letters indicate that Nietzsche had begun to cast aside the Hanslickian approach to music (in the pure contemplation of its forms), and with it also the emotion-free objectivity described by Schopenhauer; he now allowed himself to be engulfed in a sensuous experience, to be hypnotized, as it were, by the elemental power of Wagnerian music, although he was still clearly drawn to the more traditional vitality of the *Meistersinger* overture. The frequency with which Nietzsche invoked the name of Schopenhauer as he entered his Wagnerian phase should, however, not be allowed to obscure an essential irrelevance of this philosophy to his "conversion." For Schopenhauer's central aesthetic principle was the liberation from all faculties closely associated with the Will in order that the intellect might function in supreme indifference to the otherwise insistent world of pain, pleasure and desire, the palpable manifestations of the metaphysical Will. In the aesthetic experience, according to Schopenhauer, this state was to be achieved only briefly; one must look to the genius or the saint to find it permanently realized: in the genius by reason of a native overbalance of the faculty of intellect, and in the saint through ascetic suppression of the erotic impulse, Schopenhauer's seat of the Will.

Schopenhauer was not a mystic, since the highest form of existence sought after by him lay in the *release* of the individual from bondage to any underlying metaphysical unity, not the reverse. Nietzsche's concept of the Dionysian, when fully formulated, implied a renewed contact of the individual, through the art of music, with the sphere from which he had been expelled, a submerging of the consciously thinking being in the primitive life-giving chaos ("der ewige Urschmerz"). As of the fall of 1868 this characteristic distinction had not even affected Nietzsche's terminology, and he continued to express himself in the manner of a Schopenhauerian. With the insecurity of a creative thinker not yet prepared to declare his independence, he still identified himself with an image of his mentor, but in reality had distorted the image of Schopenhauer after his own likeness. It was Nietzsche who harbored mystical tendencies, yet he was pleased to refer to Schopenhauer as "der große Mystagoge" (HKB II, 310); it was Wagner's music which finally permitted him to mature his concept of the Dionysian, yet he could think of no better term for it in December 1868 than "dieses Schopenhauerische Tonmeer" (HKB II, 280).

Schopenhauer's aesthetics of music had been based primarily on his rather primitive notions of the works of Mozart, Rossini, and possibly Beethoven; only a restlessly creative mind could have stretched it to cover the kind of experiences Nietzsche reported as he moved into his Wagnerian phase, while unaware of the essential distortion involved. Some two years later, however, when Nietzsche had progressed farther in the development of his own aesthetic terminology, he referred to Bach's *Matthäuspassion* – for which he felt intense intellectual admiration ("unermeßliche Verwunderung" was the expression used), rather than any semi-mystical intoxication – as "die Musik der Verneinung des Willens" (HKB III, 51). In preferring for Bach the old Schopenhauerian terminology rather than his newer "Dionysian" vocabulary, he now demonstrated awareness of the gulf between these two kinds of aesthetic experience.

If Nietzsche was guilty on the one hand of burdening Schopenhauer's concepts with his own meaning, he was also, in the few months prior to his first meeting with Wagner, beginning to associate the philosopher and the composer in a very functional, although misleading, sense. The two names now frequently appear together in Nietzsche's correspondence, and it is this juxtaposition which strongly suggests that Schopenhauer played a significant role in Nietzsche's conversion to Wagner. Were however such a conclusion justified, there must necessarily have been some slight evidence of their interplay before the transitional stage in question. Nietzsche does not in fact refer to Wagner and Schopenhauer together until his letter to Sophie Ritschl of July 2, 1868, at a moment when his original Schopenhauer enthusiasm has ceased to be productive. Until his first conversation with Wagner Nietzsche had no way of knowing that the composer himself was enamoured of the philosopher of pessimism, apart from the unlikely event that he had seen through the eroticized precipitate of that philosophy in *Tristan und Isolde*. Nietzsche, it would seem, began to associate them spontaneously, and for reasons best understood by the student of the psyche.

For him Schopenhauer had filled the role of moral preceptor, teacher and, in the absence of any living male parent, perhaps even of spiritual father. But Schopenhauer's metaphysics seen as a coherent system had been intellectually relegated to the harmless category of "Begriffsdichtung," and what remainder Nietzsche had chosen to appropriate was being deformed in his own image. Metaphorically, the father had been devoured by the son. Wagner, who ultimately served much the same function for Nietzsche in hastening the maturing process, now loomed on Nietzsche's horizon as the new warrior against the intellectual and cultural status quo. Here was a living genius with whom he could ally himself at least spiritually, if not personally, in his dissatisfaction with a mediocre environment. The obvious artistic mastery of *Die Meistersinger* as well as its theme of natural genius versus entrenched mediocrity could well have nourished such a feeling in Nietzsche, which would not at all have been dampened by the aura of rumor and mystery emanating from Wagner's feverish "public" activities and his various "incognito" journeyings. Early in the fall of 1868 Nietzsche laid plans for penetrating the inner circle of Wagner's relatives in Leipzig; he wrote to Rohde on October 8:

Im Übrigen nehme ich mir vor, etwas mehr Gesellschaftsmensch zu werden: insbesondre habe ich eine Frau aufs Korn genommen, von der mir Wunderdinge erzählt sind, die Frau des Professor Brockhaus, Schwester Richard Wagners: über deren Capacitäten Freund Windisch... eine erstaunliche Meinung hat. (HKB II, 245)

In the same letter Nietzsche related Schopenhauer to Wagner in a kind of equation: "...mir behagt an Wagner, was mir an Schopenhauer behagt, die ethische Luft, der faustische Duft, Kreuz, Tod und Gruft etc." (HKB II, 246). Clearly the conception of Schopenhauer underlying this comparison is not that of the stubborn metaphysician of the Will, nor of the prophet of the ascetic life, but that of the idealized hero who scorns all obstacles in his striving to master his existence, a shining and fearless warrior in an indifferent or hostile world, not unlike Dürer's "Knight with Death and the Devil," long one of Nietzsche's favorite prints. But the warrior image was already more appropriate to the real Wagner than to Schopenhauer, whose Faustian heroism was perhaps less evident in actual life than in the literary image he projected for Nietzsche. Significantly, the latter presented Wagner with a copy of this engraving at Christmas in 1870 (HKB III, 99). The sympathetic Schopenhauer-Wagner equation was however immediately provoked by his reading of Otto Jahn's smugly rationalistic critiques of *Tannhäuser* and *Lohengrin*[30] in the fall of 1868; from Nietzsche's remarks at that time one can already visualize the battle lines that would be drawn once the two men had joined forces.

Ich gebe ihm [Jahn] trotzdem vielfach Recht, insbesondre darin, daß er Wagner für den Repräsentanten eines modernen, alle Kunstinteressen in sich aufsaugenden und verdauenden Dilettantismus hält; aber gerade von diesem Standpunkte aus kann man nicht genug staunen, wie bedeutend jede einzelne Kunstanlage in diesem Menschen ist, welche unverwüstliche Energie hier mit vielseitigen künstlerischen Talenten gepaart ist: während die "Bildung," je bunter und umfassender sie zu sein pflegt, gewöhnlich mit mattem Blicke, schwachen Beinen und entnervten Lenden auftritt. (HKB II, 246)

Inwardly Nietzsche was thus fully prepared to capitulate to the spell of the artist himself whenever they should meet. Presently a combination of circumstances took care of that detail, too. Not in vain had Nietzsche played the "Prize-Song" for Sophie Ritschl, as it provided her the cue needed to bring the name of her young friend into the conversation with Richard Wagner during one of the latter's incognito visits with the Brockhaus family. Wagner showed sudden interest in the young philologist versed in his music; a meeting was soon arranged, and it was reported by Nietzsche in detail in the oft-quoted letter to Rohde of November 9, 1868. It was his first encounter with living genius, and the letter shows him to have been quite overcome by Wagner's display of wit, temperament, boisterous charm and enthusiasm, not the least of which was for Schopenhauer.

If Nietzsche was less able to hold his own in matters of Wagner's music, his intimate knowledge of Schopenhauer's thought gave him ample means to impress. Thus Wagner's prompt invitation to call on him at Tribschen "um Musik und Philosophie zu treiben" (HKB II, 268). The unexpected summons to fill a vacancy at Basel a few months later was to make that possible for Nietzsche too, as well as the twenty-two subsequent visits with the Wagners at their home near the Lake of Lucerne.

For a time at least the name of Schopenhauer was to figure prominently in their friendship. In Wagner's case the discussions with Nietzsche apparently occasioned an intensified concern with the aesthetics of Schopenhauer, which, according to a recent study,[31] had already begun to effect a modification of Wagner's music-dramatic theory as early as 1861. The culmination of this development, which involved mainly the relative weight of drama versus music, is to be found in the "Beethoven" essay of 1870. For Nietzsche this was an encouragement to continue wearing the garb of a Schopenhauerian, much as he had done earlier for the sake of Rohde and other friends. Seen in retrospect, the relationship with Wagner decidedly fostered Nietzsche's development as a cultural psychologist, but in the period at hand the prolonged dealings with the philosopher of Wagner's choice merely contributed to the rank confusion, in *Die Geburt der Tragödie*, of Schopenhauerian and specifically Nietzschean concepts. It was a case in which a young author's awareness of the tastes of his first and most sympathetic readers played an insidious role in the shaping of his work. If Nietzsche was thus far unable to free his own writing of the unassimilated vestiges of Schopenhauer's philosophy, it is scarcely surprising that he proved incapable of conceiving Schopenhauer's personality as distinct from his own. *Schopenhauer als Erzieher* (1874), apparently written in good faith as a grateful portrayal of the older philosopher, is clearly a projection of Nietzsche himself, a fact the author recognized only years later (*cf.* XV, 51).

As for Wagner's music, it can be stated unequivocally that *Die Meistersinger* was the only one of the mature works which Nietzsche acquired fully on his own and the one which he knew best from actual performance. Probably the most eloquent bit of prose on Wagner's music in all of his writings is the section (§240) in *Jenseits von Gut und Böse* that he wrote on rehearing the prelude. In January 1869 Nietzsche journeyed to Dresden especially to attend the local premiere of *Die Meistersinger*, and his last musical "act" before settling down at his new post in Basel a few months later was his attendance at a performance in Karlsruhe under the direction of the rising young Wagnerian conductor Hermann Levi. As far as the records show, this was the last operatic performance of any kind for Nietzsche until June 1872. Basel had no such highly developed monument to dramatic culture as an opera house, and in any case Wagnerian works would have been the very last to be produced there. During the first years there Nietzsche was very much the conscientious professor who scarcely left town, apart from his visits to Tribschen. One exception to this restricted life, his attendance at Wagner's concert for the Mannheim *Wagnerverein* on December 20, 1871,[32] inspired in a letter to Rohde the following comment, in which the shift away from Schopenhauerian terminology toward his own is now obvious:

> Mir gieng es wie einem, dem eine Ahnung sich endlich erfüllt. Denn genau das ist Musik und nichts sonst! Und genau das meine ich mit dem Wort "Musik," wenn ich das Dionysische schildere, und nichts sonst! (HKB III, 178)

This single musical excursion was followed in June 1872 by Nietzsche's visit to Munich, when Hans von Bülow gave the European musical public its second chance to experience a production of *Tristan*. What is seldom sufficiently stressed is that this was Nietzsche's first and only opportunity to evaluate in actual performance (he heard it twice) a work to which he had been introduced more than a decade earlier. Apart from a brief technical interest in the chromatic idiom, he had given little indication of enduring fondness for the work in that interval. The intervening association with the Wagners had obviously done something to condition Nietzsche for what he termed "[den] erhabensten Kunsteindruck meines Lebens" (HKB

III, 263). By his own admission in the summer of 1872, he had not yet heard *Lohengrin* and *Der fliegende Holländer* (HKB III, 274), and did not do so later.

But *Die Geburt der Tragödie*, which included in its final version an eloquent passage on the third act of *Tristan*, was in the hands of the printer before either of these excursions from Basel. Thus Nietzsche's most blatantly Wagnerian propaganda was in large degree the product of a fertile imagination working with scores and a piano under the suggestive influence of the composer himself. Curiously enough, Nietzsche now chose to praise not the climactic second act of *Tristan* (which had appealed to Krug), but the third act with its long sections of tedious declamation, which he described "als ungeheuren symphonischen Satz" (I, 176). It can be clearly shown that some of Wagner's opinions and prejudices about other music and musicians influenced Nietzsche in this period,[33] and it is reasonable to suppose that here too the conversations with the composer who viewed himself as the successor to Beethoven were responsible for this insight so far removed from anything we might have expected from Nietzsche. Indeed Wagner himself must have opened his mind to the deeper meaning of his most radical work, and as the special object of such intellectual and aesthetic intimacies it was *Tristan* which then became for Nietzsche the permanent symbol of his unforgettable Tribschen experience. Abstracted to the status of a symbol it could than remain unsullied and untarnished long after the harmonious and productive days of his friendship with Wagner were over. Nietzsche never attacked or criticized it later, even in his most satiric moments. Perhaps it was crucial that he did not again hear the work performed; he was thus at no time constrained to revise the meaning of this personal symbol. To a lesser extent the process may have been repeated in the case of the later *Ring* operas, especially *Die Götterdämmerung*, on which Wagner was at work during the last years of the Tribschen period. If we may draw any conclusion from Nietzsche's overly hopeful expectations as the opening Bayreuth festival drew near in 1876, it might be that he attached an exaggerated subjective meaning to the artistic product of the years of his most intimate friendship with Wagner – so exaggerated that it could not survive objective analysis. Nietzsche's attendance at the production of an entire *Ring* cycle and some of the rehearsals at this point in his deteriorating personal relations with Wagner, and at this level of his now steadily decreasing physical tolerance for such experiences, merely brought home to him the inescapable realization that no act of personal magnanimity, no attitude of indulgent idealism on his part could close the widening breach between them. As if to save the few meaningful remnants left to him after Bayreuth, he instinctively refrained from further Wagnerian "exposures."

VI. "DER MELOMANE"

We do not propose to retell in these pages the story of Nietzsche's friendship with Wagner, or to review the better known evidence of the slow erosion in their mutual confidence following Wagner's move to Wahnfried – all of which has been sufficiently treated in the Nietzsche literature.[34] This friendship stands as the most significant chapter in Nietzsche's growth into a creative philosopher, and its importance derives mainly from its necessary destruction. For his acceptance of the end of this relationship marked the beginning of his first real independence of oppressive intellectual forebears and further provided him with the motivation to diagnose the condition of modern European culture as reflected in the Wagnerian phenomenon and his own personal involvement with it.

Instead, our focus is again on Nietzsche's little known musical output in this, the final period of his activity as a composer. When we previously attempted to demonstrate the momentary interest in Wagner through a study of the stylistic impact of *Tristan und Isolde* on Nietzsche's early compositions, to some extent we merely presumed the right to do so. In the later period, where we are better informed as to Nietzsche's attitudes toward Wagner through literary documents, the compositions clearly reflect a parallel fluctuation of sympathy and antipathy in what amounts to a justification for our earlier presumption. Once again Nietzsche completes the cycle of acceptance and rejection, but now it is slower and vastly more complicated by the personal element of his relationship with Wagner.

Four works of some scope and consequence have been preserved from this period, works composed between November 1871 and November 1873. Unfortunately the new composition which Nietzsche mentioned to Rohde in the summer of 1868, as he was entering the Wagnerian phase, has not survived (*cf.* HKB II, 230 and note, HKB II, 455), and the same appears to be true of the "Kyrie" composed in January 1866, although this composition was still extant at the time of the HK edition (*cf.* HK III, 397). The works we shall examine briefly are:

"Nachklang einer Sylvesternacht, mit Prozessionslied, Bauerntanz und Mitternachtsglocke" (November 1-7, 1871)
"Manfred Meditation" (April 1872)
"Monodie à deux" (early 1873)
"Hymnus auf die Freundschaft" (November 1873)

After his assumption of academic duties in Basel, Nietzsche's muse appears to have rested for more than two years, while his visits to Tribschen tended to fill out the musical aspect of his existence. He wrote to Krug that he had no intention of composing again when he set about revising "Eine Sylvesternacht," a composition dating from his school days at Pforta, so as to have a four-hand number to perform with his congenial house-mate in Basel, Professor Franz Overbeck. But in the process a new piece came into existence, one bearing only a slight resemblance in thematic material to the earlier opus. Nietzsche gave it the bizarre title listed above, and then generally referred to it as the "Silvesterklänge." Not one of his closer friends was spared the news that he had composed again, and he not only performed the piece frequently with his professorial friends, but also had a copy made especially for Bayreuth.[35] On the other hand Nietzsche was also characteristically apologetic about the work, and this ambivalent attitude accompanied all further works of this sort:

> Was thut es und wem schadet es, wenn ich mich alle 6 Jahre einmal durch eine dionysische Weise von dem Banne der Musik freikaufe! Denn so betrachte ich diesen musikalischen Exceß, als einen Freibrief. (HKB III, 162)

Nevertheless the same process was repeated a few months later, when he undertook to revise the first page of the "Silvesterklänge." Again a new piece was written down, one showing similarities in theme, but differing markedly in overall mood. This was the "Manfred Meditation," a copy of which Nietzsche was bold enough to present to Hans von Bülow, arousing thereby a veritable storm of intemperate but not totally unjustified criticism (cf. GB III, 349-352). This is not the place to discuss the permanent musical value of

Nietzsche's creations, which Wagner and his wife accepted as a kind of "recreation" for the young professor and were generally careful not to attack. However both works are swollen in such a way that the disparity between intention and realization is all too evident. Herein lies the basic contrast with Nietzsche's most successful compositions, the more unpretentious of his Lieder. In the gloomy "Manfred" music such interpretive directions as "langsam und brütend," "sehr ausdrucksvoll," "stark und pathetisch," "klagend," "sehr feierlich und langsam," "zart und geheimnisvoll" – appear as compensations for qualities basically lacking in the musical realization. But one does not need to search hard to find the imprint of Wagner in either work. Although there are no identifiable quotations from Wagner's music, there are more than a few instances of thematic parallels and borrowed techniques. Compared with the rather clumsy and thick chords of the early tone poem "Ermanarich," the harmonies here are less dramatically dissonant, yet on the whole richer, smoother and more sonorous in the Wagnerian manner. As in Wagner's advanced idiom dissonance is more often than not the product of a fluid chromatic counterpoint or melodic interweaving; the greatest dissonances are approached and resolved logically by way of harmonies of lower order dissonance. If in our time Wagner's dissonance is no longer distinctly felt as such, this is at least partially due to his orderly patterns of relative dissonance values, as contrasted with the chaotic harmonic experimentation to be found here and there in Nietzsche's "expressionistic" tone poem "Ermanarich."

Two Wagnerian mannerisms which have crept into these pieces are the pedal point and the harmonic sequence, both of which are staples in Wagner's recipe for extended musical climaxes such as that of the "Liebesnacht." They are related and often used in conjunction by Wagner in his repetitive technique. In the former a motif is repeated with changing harmonic intensity over a single bass tone, and in the latter the entire harmonic support shifts with each repetition. Wagner did not invent these techniques, but his characteristic method of using them was unmistakably aped by Nietzsche. Further, both of these pieces are written in triple meter, and it appears not entirely coincidental that Nietzsche is so fond of sequential repetitions of the dotted figure |♩. ♫| or |♩. ♪♫| in melodic configurations reminiscent of the quieter love music in act two of *Tristan* (*cf.* p. 185 ff. of the Peters vocal score). Common Wagnerian clichés to be found in Nietzsche's melodic line are the "turns" preceding a leap upward of a fifth or sixth and the typical jumbling of double and triple subdivisions of the main rhythmic pulse, usually with the effect of slowing the tempo toward the end of a measure by quickening the melodic motion:

(Wagner)　　　(Nietzsche)

Such Wagnerian idiosyncrasies are to be found rather more frequently in the slow sections of the "Silvesterklänge" than in the later piece, which gains something approaching a "classical" effect through the introduction of a descending "Mannheim rocket" (arpeggio theme) about half way through, with attendant tonic-dominant key relationships. Yet the opening motif of the "Manfred Meditation" ("sehr ausdrucksvoll") reflects even the shape of the opening line of the *Tristan* prelude, an upward leap followed by descending chromatics. In neither piece, however, do the various elements add up to a clear musical style; rather we are served a potpourri of advanced and conservative practice, of the banal and the inspired, of the noisy and the delicate, all strung together as though illustrating a text which is not supplied. The tonal anarchy which reigns here must not, in all fairness, be imputed to Wagner, although his example did little to counteract Nietzsche's tendency in this direction. Such pieces as these, although not without their impressive moments, tend to demonstrate Nietzsche's weaknesses as a composer with embarrassing clarity. Here the musical imagination or gift for combination far over-reaches any powers of musical organization he may have had. Short motifs dominate, and with the total absence of more spacious melody or a compelling logical structure, the pieces never gain sufficient momentum to become convincing. Indeed something of Wagner's leitmotiv technique may be involved here, but Nietzsche had not progressed beyond the exterior manifestations. Bülow's comment is brusque but merited: "...eine in Erinnerungsschwelgerei an Wagner'sche Klänge taumelnde Phantasie ist keine Produktionsbasis" (GB III, 350). Further comment on the two compositions dating from the Tribschen period of Nietzsche's friendship with Wagner would be superfluous.

If Nietzsche had suffered any irreparable damage to his ego through Bülow's critique (he swore off composition for another six years in a letter to Krug [HKB III, 267]), the marriage of Olga Herzen and Gabriel Monod early in 1873 appeared made to order as a fresh enticement for the composer to indulge his muse after all. The opportunity to pun proved irresistible, for nothing less than "Une Monodie à deux" emerged as Nietzsche's contribution to the occasion. Once again he had unearthed a youthful work which became the nucleus of a new piano duet. The beginning of the piece is identical with that of the "Verkündigung Mariae" from his old oratorio, but Nietzsche goes on to enrich the thematic material, to rebuild the piece in an integrated tripartite form, and to conclude it with an imposing plagal cadence.[36] The "Monodie" remains noticeable free of the ambiguous Wagnerian harmonies of his earlier works, and there is only one measure (in ninety-five) of real chromaticism, here a simple product of the voice-leading. Only the new theme or motif could be termed Wagner-inspired, and this again because it rhythmically parallels one of the insistent motifs in the prelude to *Tristan* (𝅘𝅥𝅮𝅘𝅥𝅮𝅘𝅥 𝅘𝅥𝅮𝅘𝅥𝅮𝅘𝅥) and follows the melodic contour of its first four notes. But in the harmonic movement, which in the case of a simple theme may be more characteristic than the theme itself, the resemblance ends: Wagner's fourth tone is an appoggiatura, while in Nietzsche's motif it is a chord tone. Although the evidence in this piece is still inconclusive, it clearly suggests a step out from under the shadow of Wagner toward a more traditional concept of structure and harmony.

This tendency is definitely shown to be a trend in Nietzsche's next, and for all purposes, last composition,[37] completed late the same year (HKB IV, 31). The "Hymnus auf die Freundschaft" consists of three strophes, with a prelude and two extended interludes. It exists in various arrangements for piano solo or duet, and in most versions the several sections are provided with fanciful titles. The relationship of music and word, which in any case is slight, does not concern us here. The musical center of gravity, the "Hymnus" proper, is a majestic movement, dark and weighty in character, but not without flashes of brighter harmonies at times suggestive of Brahms. Although characteristically late romantic, there are few chromatic progressions, and these are the harmonies which can be found in Brahms's mature style as well as in Wagner's. The few chromatic passages, moreover, are concentrated (perhaps meaningfully!) in the section entitled

"Wie in glücklich trauriger Erinnerung." In place of the Wagnerian mannerisms, we hear, in this rather pianistic work, the familiar echoes of Chopin or Schumann, and the tonality is centered (D major) in a way foreign to either the "Silvesterklänge" or "Manfred." But Nietzsche has not suddenly become a great or even a good composer, and the prelude and the interludes contain a good deal of insignificant fill-in material, a derivative, no doubt, of Nietzsche's ramblings at the keyboard. The variation form to which Nietzsche has turned here is a solid principle of traditional musical organization, and if the contrapuntal embellishments of the chorale are awkward and amateurish, the composer's good intentions are everywhere in evidence. More subtle formally are the hidden variations and anticipations of the chorale tune in the prelude and the interludes. For all its faults this music manages to sound better than a cursory glance at the score might lead one to expect. For Nietzsche himself the chorale never lost its moving appeal, and it seemed worthy enough in later years to be tailored to accompany a poem by Lou Salomé, the "Hymnus an das Leben," although perhaps unduly somber in that context. In Bayreuth the piece produced little joy, and may even have suggested to the suspicious Wagner that Nietzsche was now going over into the enemy camp. At least an entry in Cosima's diary points to this possibility, for after recounting an amusing story about the "Silvesterklänge" she wrote: "Leider aber kann ich über das Thema nicht mehr lachen, denn ein 'Hymnus an [*sic*] die Freundschaft' hat eigentlich den Bruch begonnen, der kam nach Bayreuth und war sehr traurig. ..."[38] Nietzsche, who did not return to Bayreuth after the completion of this piece until August 1874, or about ten months later, may well have sent a copy in advance of his arrival there, just as he had previously provided copies of the "Silvesterklänge" and the "Manfred Meditation."

VII. RUPTURE

No particular effort of the intuitive imagination is required to see that the musical characteristics of the "Hymnus auf die Freundschaft" stand in a relationship to other aspects of Nietzsche's friendship with Wagner which cannot be mere coincidence. At the personal level, for instance, there was the growing tendency, after the laying of the cornerstone in Bayreuth in 1872, for Nietzsche to resist further engulfment in the Wagnerian project as a necessary defense of his own individuality. The Tribschen phase of their friendship had been marked by great warmth, high idealism, and the sense of sharing creatively on a level denied to the valley-dwellers of European culture. For Wagner this was but a brief respite from the more practical worries associated with his grandiose theatrical plans, while Nietzsche was essentially at home only in the rarified atmosphere of the intellectual life. Even by the end of 1872 he had second thoughts about stopping off in Bayreuth on his way back from Naumburg. His explanation to Gersdorff for his failure to appear is most revealing:

> Aber in kleinen untergeordneten Nebenpunkten und in einer gewissen für mich nothwendigen beinahe "sanitarisch" zu nennenden Enthaltung von *häufigerem* persönlichen Zusammenleben muß ich mir eine Freiheit wahren, wirklich nur um jene Treue in einem höheren Sinne halten zu können. (HKB III, 361)

A scant year later Nietzsche's attempt to analyze

without sentiment the reasons for the continuing crisis in Bayreuth produced a sheaf of notes scarcely charitable toward the assertive personality of Wagner and the aesthetic principles which were its precipitate. These were but tiny eruptions of a large-scale subterranean process; Nietzsche begged Gersdorff to keep silent on the matter, and the critical notes of January 1874 were laid away in the bottom of his desk, unseen by anyone until years later.[39] Yet in the outlet open to him in his music Nietzsche could not so readily disengage his official and his private views; the fluctuating eclecticism of his compositions reflects with greater honesty than any remarks to his friends the changing focus of his musical interests. It is also symptomatic of this disparity that about the same time, the professed Wagnerian Friedrich Nietzsche exhibited an undue interest in Brahms's *Triumphlied*, a rather Handelian work for double chorus. Although Nietzsche refrained from any clear statement about this music, he nevertheless looked repeatedly for an opportunity to hear it performed (*cf.* HKB IV, 62, 82). Late in 1874 he even took along the score to Bayreuth, as if to test Wagner's own reaction to it. "Das rote Buch" caused a scene there which might easily have been predicted.[40]

It is unlikely for chronological reasons alone that there was any specifically Brahmsian "influence" on Nietzsche's "Hymnus," although one might suspect it from the sonorities of the work.[41] It was rather a question of parallel interest displayed by Nietzsche in the conservative musical elements of periodic melody, clear tonality, and old-fashioned counterpoint in his own composition and in the work of one of Wagner's enemies. The "Hymnus" can be seen as a reaching back toward elements of his earliest contrapuntal exercises and the Lieder of Pforta days which had generally disappeared from his music with the onset of his personal relationship with Wagner; as an attempt to work again within the framework of the structural principles missing or obscured in Wagner's music. In this Nietzsche had completed the cycle back to a traditionalist view for the second time in a dozen years. There is no indication that he ever departed from it again – at least not before the confused final months of his productive life.

A recent study by Curt von Westernhagen[42] attempts to trace the rupture with Wagner to petty personal differences between them, reviving the time-worn (and unreliable) reports of Wagner's abusive critiques of Nietzsche's compositions, and claiming to produce evidence of an even more telling affront to Nietzsche's ego – to which the author ascribes Nietzsche's later "viciousness" toward the Master. Most of this can be countered, if not incontrovertibly refuted, by anyone with a proper appreciation of Nietzsche as a thinker and as a human being. Westernhagen's analysis, which warms over the same hash of quotations served up by him over twenty-five years ago,[43] could only result from the provincial assumption that no one of Nietzsche's intelligence could conceivably part company with the great master of Bayreuth unless it were for crassly human-all-too-human reasons and an improper notion of the stature of Wagner's art to begin with. In suggesting that Nietzsche never really understood Wagner's music Westernhagen perhaps comes as close to a just estimate of the matter as is possible for a devoted Wagnerian apologist. For if anything becomes clear in the present investigation, it is that Wagner's music remained for Nietzsche an unsolved problem from first to last, a problem that was temporarily suppressed during the period of his closest association with the composer, and perhaps for reasons having little to do with music as such.

While surveying his youthful compositions during a visit home at the end of 1874, Nietzsche was struck by the overall stability of his musical style:

> Es bleibt mir ewig sonderbar, wie in der Musik die Unveränderlichkeit des Charakters sich offenbart; was ein Knabe in ihr ausspricht, ist so deutlich die Sprache des Grundwesens seiner ganzen Natur, daß auch der Mann daran nichts geändert wünscht – natürlich die Unvollkommenheit der Technik und s. w. abgerechnet. (HKB IV, 136; GB III, 476)

Such an observation could not have been made a few years earlier, in the period of the "Silvesterklänge" and the "Manfred Meditation." What surprised Nietzsche now was the unsuspected proximity of his "Hymnus auf die Freundschaft" to the elegiac lyricism of his best Lieder and to the traditional polyphonic techniques last employed in his music with any consistency in the early days of the "Germania." In retrospect he could observe that he had once again returned, after a brief struggle with the demon of modernism, to the area of his natural inspiration, a tradition-bound romantic lyricism – in what amounted to a reaffirmation of the consistency of his musical character. We may go even further. It is likely not only that his musical creativity was strongest in this limited conservative vein, but also that his basic musical taste was similarly restricted. Handel provided the first overpowering musical experience; the persistence of Schumann as the favored composer well beyond his adolescence, despite all traffic with "Zukunftsmusik," points further in the same direction. Nietzsche became a "Wagnerian" not, as he insisted later, through the influence of the work he had known the longest – *Tristan* – but rather by way of that opera in which Wagner consciously combined his mature style with the musical techniques of the past, in flagrant violation of most of his own theories of music drama: *Die Meistersinger.* When Nietzsche began to reassert his musical independence, it was the traditionalist music of Brahms from which he attempted to derive moral support. The analogy might be further developed. However, it would be too easy to explain Nietzsche's Bayreuth experience in 1876 and his later musical preferences in terms of a simple continuation of this pattern of conservatism. For it is clear that illness with its complex and disturbing effects on Nietzsche's musical sensibilities began to play a significant role not later than 1875. Unfortunately this problem cannot adequately be treated in these pages. But we may nonetheless observe that Nietzsche's musical appetites in the years of his greatest philosophical productivity were satisfied mainly by music of clear formal proportion, rhythmic vitality, harmonic elegance and melodic charm: music provided in large part by Chopin, Bizet, and Peter Gast. It is likely that Nietzsche's illness merely accelerated an already vigorous trend back toward the conservatism he had deserted a few years earlier, that it aided him in stripping away what was essentially foreign to his nature. If this is so, then Nietzsche's infatuation with Wagnerian music, quite apart from any evaluation of his friendship with Wagner, may indeed be regarded as an aberration.

In his ultimate view Nietzsche would have us understand the break with Wagner and Wagnerian art as the return to health of the modern European steeped since childhood in the waters of European decadence par excellence – Wagnerian music – and therefore best equipped to pass judgment on this phenomenon. In reality Nietzsche can scarcely be described as a Wagnerian at all until the last year of his university study. Whether Wagner is in fact more decadent than Mozart, Schubert, Brahms or our current wave of twelve-tone composers, may long remain a matter for discussion. But much as

RUPTURE

Nietzsche had once turned the harmless old David Friedrich Strauss into a bugbear of nineteenth-century complacency and optimism, so too did his peculiarly concrete manner of cultural analysis now require a focus and a target in a personality such as Wagner's. To this requirement we may attribute in large measure the dramatic oversimplification in Nietzsche's portrayal of the central intellectual, aesthetic, and personal event of his life to be found in *Ecce homo* and other late works. Perhaps the present study will have succeeded in demonstrating how considerable is the distortion involved in Nietzsche's image of himself as a Wagnerian, how fragile the myth which persists in the popular imagination.

NOTES

[1] All references to works frequently cited are carried in the text. See list of abbreviations.

[2] See T. Moody Campbell, "Nietzsche – Wagner to 1872," *PMLA*, LVI (1941), 544-577, and Richard Blunck, *Nietzsche* (Basel, 1953), pp. 69-70. Both writers base their findings on the *Historisch-kritische Gesamtausgabe* and thus avoid some of the guesswork of their predecessors. In his concentration on the theory of the music drama Campbell of necessity neglects all other aspects of the Nietzsche-Wagner relationship; their agreement or disagreement about the function of text and music, however interesting, is insufficient to explain either their friendship or its subsequent collapse. Without elaborating the thesis Campbell speculates that Nietzsche was musically a "classicist" who was briefly displaced from his true center under the personal influence of Wagner (p. 547). The statement lacks documentation or qualification. Blunck on the other hand does little more than point to the contradictory evidence found in the published documents, and defers comment on Nietzsche's musical compositions, the only other possible source, until their publication.

[3] Apart from the *Hymnus an das Leben*, published by Fritzsch at Nietzsche's request in 1887, the only compositions ever published are found in Elisabeth Förster-Nietzsche, *Das Leben Friedrich Nietzsches*, Vol. I (two brief samples), *Nietzsches musikalische Werke*, ed. Georg Göhler, Vol. I (Leipzig, 1924): "Lieder für eine Singstimme mit Klavierbegleitung," and in Gustav Lenzewski, "Nietzsche und Wagner," *Die Meistersinger von Nürnberg* (Programmheft der Bayreuther Festspiele, 1959), p. 21 ("Der Tod der Könige"). All other compositions by Nietzsche discussed in the present monograph are unpublished. See the acknowledgments in the preface.

[4] See Gustav Krug, *Vier Gesänge für eine Singstimme mit Pianofortebegleitung*, Leipzig: Breitkopf und Härtel, n.d.

[5] *Cf. Das Kunstwerk der Zukunft*, Chapter II: "Oratorien

– diese geschlechtslosen Opernembryonen!" – "...die naturwidrige Ausgeburt des Oratoriums..." (*Gesammelte Schriften* III, 131, 141).

[6] Originally published in 1851 in an edition of 500 copies, *Oper und Drama* was not read by Nietzsche until the appearance of a second edition in 1868. His reaction then was clearly that of the neophyte (*cf.* HKB II, 273 f.). T. Moody Campbell (*op. cit.* [note 2], p. 545) and Hans Wolff (*Nietzsche* [Bern, 1956], p. 20) find a vaguely parallel passage in one of Nietzsche's school essays of 1864, but this can only be a coincidence. The passage in question fails to indicate any concern on Nietzsche's part with Wagner's main thesis, the dramatic aspect of the amalgamation of the arts.

[7] By appending it to Nietzsche's letter home of November 19, 1862, the editors of the HK imply a later composition of Krug's letter than is warranted by internal evidence (allusion to Wagner's attempt to produce *Tristan* in Vienna). They were presumably misled by Krug's erroneous dating of the letter "Donnerst. d. 27 November," which would by itself indicate the year 1862.

[8] Campbell (*op. cit.*, p. 544) is undoubtedly correct in emphasizing the close relationship of the separately printed notes on "das Wesen der Musik" (HK II, 89 and 114), which form an all but grammatical continuity of thought and style. Not only the rhetoric is unusual, but also the repetition of the singular intimate pronoun, otherwise unparalleled in the notes: "...wenn du nun glaubst, vor einem Marionettentheater zu stehen..." – "...wenn du über die lächeltest, die in solchem Formenwerk leben konnten..." – "...wenn du wie niedergeschmettert von der Macht der Musik vor den leidenschaftlichen Wogen Tristan und Isoldes dastehst..." Neither mirth over the admirers of the fugue nor helplessness in the face of the *Tristan* music appears to have been characteristic of Nietzsche himself at the time, and the rhetorical exaggeration further-

more suggests that it was addressed to one or more of his friends. A later reference to this lost essay corroborates this interpretation: "...vor zwei Jahren, als ich mehere [sic] Bogen über diesen Gegenstand an meine Freunde schrieb..." (HKB I, 255). What we have here are then patently notes for an argument with close friends, and not the self-analysis seen in these lines by Blunck (*op. cit.*, p. 69 f.). Nietzsche was never reluctant to use the first person pronoun when he meant it.

[9] Jack Stein, *Richard Wagner and the Synthesis of the Arts* (Detroit, 1960), p. 68.

[10] A characteristic excerpt from his "Altera commentarii pars" ("Gedanken über die chorische Musik in der Tragödie...") in the "Primum Oedipodis regis carmen choricum" of 1864: "Es ist sicherlich eine gegründete Vermuthung, wenn ich annehme, daß zur Blütezeit der Tragoedie auch die musikalischen Elemente zusammen nach einen [sic] einheitlichen Plan geordnet, daß Ordnung und Ebenmaß der musikalischen Glieder sowohl in der ganzen Tragoedie als in jedem einzelnen Chorliede herrschte" (HK II, 375).

[11] See H. M. Wolff, pp. 13-17; and Blunck, pp. 75 ff.

[12] The title page reads: "J. G. Albrechtsberger's sämmtliche Schriften über Generalbaß, Harmonielehre, und Tonsetzkunst; zum Selbstunterricht. Systematisch geordnet, mit zahlreichen, aus dessen mündlichen Mittheilungen geschöpften Erläuterungs-Beyspielen, und einer kurzen Anleitung zum Partitur-Spiel, nebst Beschreibung aller bis jetzt gebräuchlichen Instrumente. Vermehrt und herausgegeben von seinem Schüler Ignaz, Ritter von Seyfried. 3 Bde. Zweyte, revidirte Auflage, Wien 1837."

[13] In the exposition of one of the longest fugues in his "Weihnachtsoratorium" the subject enters at intervals of the second above, the sixth below, and finally the ninth below the original statement.

[14] See note 3.

[15] Karl Fortlage, *Das musikalische System der Griechen in seiner Urgestalt*, Leipzig, 1847. August Reissmann, *Allgemeine Geschichte der Musik*, 3 vols. Munich, 1863-64; and *Robert Schumann: Sein Leben und seine Werke*, Berlin, 1865. Adolf Bernhard Marx, *Ludwig van Beethoven: Leben und Schaffen*, 2 vols. Berlin, 1859.

[16] *Nietzsches Bibliothek*, ed. Max Oehler. Vierzehnte Jahresgabe der Gesellschaft der Freunde des Nietzsche-Archivs, Weimar, 1942.

[17] *Cf.* Hanslick: "*Was* kann also die Musik von den Gefühlen darstellen, wo nicht deren Inhalt? Nur das *Dynamische* derselben. Sie vermag die Bewegung eines psychischen Vorganges nach den Momenten: schnell, langsam, stark, schwach, steigend, fallend nachzubilden. Bewegung ist aber nur *eine* Eigenschaft, *ein* Moment des Gefühls, nicht dieses selbst... Was uns außerdem in der Musik bestimmte Seelenzustände zu malen scheint, ist durchaus *symbolisch*. ... Ein anderes Mittel zu dem angeblichen Zweck, außer der Analogie der Bewegung und der Symbolik der Töne, hat die reine Musik nicht" (pp. 21-23). Nietzsche: "Die Musik ist analog dem Gefühl, nicht identisch oder Sprache des Gefühls. Das Ziel der Musik, alles Bewegte in der Natur umzusetzen in die Bewegung der Töne" (HK III, 98).

[18] Hermann Deiters, *Johannes Brahms*, Leipzig, 1880.

[19] Otto Jahn, *Wolfgang Amadeus Mozart*, 4 vols. Leipzig, 1856-59.

[20] See *NZfM*, LXII (1866), 11, 89, 139.

[21] *NZfM*, LXI (1865), 433, reviews a concert of the "Euterpe" in November 1865, which featured the prelude to *Tristan* (poorly played). Nietzsche never refers to this concert in any of his correspondence.

[22] Michael Landmann, *Geist und Leben: Varia Nietzscheana* (Bonn, 1951), p. 27.

[23] Square brackets here enclose the editorial additions of the present writer.

[24] *Sokrates und die griechische Tragödie*, ed. Hans Joachim Mette, Siebente Jahresgabe der Gesellschaft der Freun-

NOTES

de des Nietzsche-Archivs (Munich, 1933), pp. 22-23.
[25] Arthur Schopenhauer, *Sämtliche Werke*, ed. Arthur Hübscher, 2nd ed. (Wiesbaden, 1946-1950), III, 463.
[26] The essentials of Hanslick's colorful polemic against the unmusical music-lover reappear in Nietzsche's subsequent attacks on the Wagnerian public, as the following samples may illustrate. Hanslick: "Das *Elementarische* der Musik, der *Klang* und die *Bewegung* ist es, was die wehrlosen Gefühle so vieler Musikfreunde in Ketten schlägt.... Indem sie das Elementarische der Musik in passiver Empfänglichkeit auf sich wirken lassen, gerathen sie in eine vage, nur durch den Charakter des Tonstücks bestimmte übersinnlich-sinnliche Erregung. Ihr Verhalten gegen die Musik ist nicht anschauend, sondern *pathologisch;* ein stetes Dämmern, Fühlen, Schwärmen, ein Hangen und Bangen in klingendem Nichts" (Hanslick, pp. 96-97). Nietzsche: "An *un*künstlerischen Menschen sich wendend, mit allen Hilfsmitteln soll gewirkt werden. Nicht auf Kunstwirkung, sondern auf Nervenwirkung ganz allgemein ist es abgesehen" (XI, 101) – "Der Wagnerianer pur sang ist unmusikalisch; er unterliegt den Elementarkräften der Musik ungefähr wie das Weib dem Willen seines Hypnotiseurs unterliegt" (XVI, 257 [*Wille zur Macht*, § 839]).
[27] London, 1874. To be sure, Francis Hueffer the "Englishman" recognized Schopenhauer's importance once Wagner had publicly confessed his debt to the philosopher in the "Beethoven" essay of 1870. Nietzsche's *Geburt der Tragödie* also rated mention in Hueffer's book (p. 19) as part of the accepted Wagner-literature.
[28] The text of this interesting and possibly important pivot in Nietzsche's turn toward Wagner, although promised to the readers of the *NZfM*, was never made available. The contents are indicated solely in the summary given by the reviewer. "Die alleinige Möglichkeit, das Drama aus seinem gegewärtigen Verfalle wieder zu heben, machte der Redner von dem Zurückgehen auf

das griechische Drama mit seinem harmonischen Zusammenwirken von Poesie, Musik und Orchestik abhängig, auf das schon der geschichtliche Verlauf der Sonderentwicklung dieser Künste als unabweisbare Forderung hingewiesen habe und bei welchem die durch jene Sonderentwicklung gewonnenen Errungenschaften der einzelnen Künste als solche dem wiedergeborenen Drama jedenfalls zu Gute kommen würden" (*NZfM*, LXIV [1868], 261). Marbach, an accomplished student of the Greek classics, may have given a new impulse to Nietzsche's own speculations along these lines. Marbach later responded to *Die Geburt der Tragödie* by sending Nietzsche his new translation of the *Oresteia* (Leipzig, 1873). *Cf.* HKB IV, 86, 286.

[29] First published in Berlin, 1859. An American version testifies to its popularity: Louis Ehlert, *Letters on Music to a Lady*, Boston, 1870.

[30] Otto Jahn, *Gesammelte Aufsätze über Musik*, 2nd ed. (Leipzig, 1867), pp. 81 ff., 327 ff.

[31] Jack Stein, *Wagner*, pp. 149 ff.

[32] The program according to Newman: "consisting of the *Magic Flute* overture, Beethoven's Seventh Symphony, the *Lohengrin* and *Meistersinger* preludes, the *Tristan* Prelude and Liebestod, and the now inevitable *Kaisermarsch*" (Newman IV, 311-312). There was also a private performance of the *Siegfried Idyll* for Cosima and a few select friends, which presumably included Nietzsche.

[33] Nietzsche's remarks to his student Louis Kelterborn, reflected in the latter's reminiscences of his years in Basel (HKB III, 379-399; HKB IV, 343-353), indicate that he overcame his earlier dislike of *Der Freischütz* and *Oberon* (*cf.* HKB I, 292) at least to the extent of recognizing in Weber an important forerunner of Wagner (HKB III, 394); that he repeated to Kelterborn the essentials of Wagner's eulogy of *Le Nozze di Figaro* (HKB III, 393) although he himself had formerly been unenthusiastic about Mozart's operas; and that he now exhibited something akin to Wagner's private scorn for

Liszt's church music. "Er [Nietzsche] nahm dem Componisten Liszt gegenüber eine ablehnende, ja direkt feindliche Haltung ein, namentlich mit Bezug auf die kirchlichen Werke desselben, sprach von Weihrauch und Goldschaum, von hohlem Flitter, von musikalischem Jesuitenstyl, von einer wunderlichen Mischung von Religiosität und Frivolität, von katholischem, undeutschem Wesen u. dgl." (HKB III, 397). This representation of Nietzsche's view in the early seventies strikingly resembles the reactions of Wagner and Cosima to a performance of Liszt's oratorio *Christus* in 1873, as reported by Newman: "They were not wholly in tune with the work, liking neither its aromatic sensuousness nor the touch of the sophisticated in its religious outlook. It was not 'German' enough for either of them. Wagner...could never quite reconcile himself to what he called the priestly element in Liszt's church music; the aroma of incense it exhaled" (Newman IV, 396).

[34] The most useful accounts remain those in Charles Andler, *Nietzsche, sa Vie et sa Pensée*, 6 vols. (Paris, 1920-31), Vol. II; P. G. Dippel, *Wagner und Nietzsche*, Bern, 1934; Elisabeth Förster-Nietzsche, *Wagner und Nietzsche zur Zeit ihrer Freundschaft*, Munich, 1915. The last mentioned item at least contains most of the correspondence between the two men.

[35] This copy, now in the Richard Wagner-Museum, Bayreuth, bears the autograph dedication: "Frau Cosima unter herzlichsten Glückwünschen gewidmet von dem Melomanen."

[36] According to a report of Peter Gast, Wagner played the piece with Nietzsche in Bayreuth. "Wagner soll dabei nach dem kirchlich klingenden Schluss gesagt haben, Nietzsche habe den armen Monods – die nicht kirchlich eingesegnet waren – nun doch noch den Papstsegen aufgedrängt" (HKB IV, 355; *cf*. GB II, 606). A photocopy of this composition was kindly furnished by Prof. Alfred Cortot, Lausanne.

[37] In the introduction to the volume of letters addressed to himself Peter Gast recalls a "Hymnus an die Einsamkeit" (GB IV, xxiii), "ein Stück voll herber Größe und Unerbittlichkeit, in das sich sirenenhaft, doch bald mit Trotz wieder abgewiesen, bestrickende *dolce*-Stellen mischten." But Gast's memory was demonstrably less than reliable over a much shorter span than the thirty-odd years involved here, and the two references to a "Hymnus auf [sic] die Einsamkeit" in previously edited letters to Rohde (GB II, 488, 537) by no means indicate that such a work was ever completed or even partially written down. Nietzsche's "Hymnus an das Leben," not a new composition at all, but a reworking of the chorale from his "Hymnus auf die Freundschaft," was not recognized as such by Gast in 1882, although he had familiarized himself with the various arrangements of the older piece only half a dozen years before.

[38] Richard du Moulin-Eckart, *Cosima Wagner*, 2 vols. (Munich, 1929-31), II, 175-176. Quoted from Dippel, *Wagner und Nietzsche*, p. 59.

[39] The first complete publication of these notes of January 1874 occurred in Vol. X (1903), the second *Nachlass* volume of the Naumann-Kröner *Werke*, edited by Ernest Holzer. But they had been quoted liberally by Elisabeth in her biography (*Leben* II [1897], 225 ff.), as they were later in *Wagner und Nietzsche zur Zeit ihrer Freundschaft* (1915). In the 1897 volume she merely presented a selection of the material; by 1915 her memory had "improved" to the point where she could reconstruct a conversation with her brother on these notes (pp. 179-180). It is unlikely that Nietzsche ever discussed this matter with any of his relatives or friends.

[40] *Wagner und Nietzsche zur Zeit ihrer Freundschaft*, pp. 203-204.

[41] Nietzsche's "Hymnus" was composed before he had heard the Brahms composition performed, and furthermore the *"Triumphlied"* – according to a sympathetic

critic – "smacks less of Brahms than of Händel in his weaker moments" (Rob't H. Schauffler, *The Unknown Brahms* [New York, 1933], pp. 353-354).

[42] Curt von Westernhagen, *Richard Wagner*, Zürich, 1956.

[43] See Curt von Westernhagen, "Nietzsche und die deutsche Musik," *Bayreuther Blätter* LIX (1936), 8-18. Also "Wagner und Nietzsche," *Die Musik*, XXVIII, No.10 (July 1936), 725-731.

LIST OF WORKS CITED

Albrechtsberger, J. G. *Sämmtliche Schriften über Generalbass, Harmonielehre, und Tonsetzkunst*...ed. Ignaz von Seyfried. 2nd ed., 3 vols. Vienna, 1837.
Andler, Charles, *Nietzsche, sa Vie et sa Pensée*. 6 vols. Paris, 1920-31.
Anregungen für Kunst, Leben und Wissenschaft, ed. Franz Brendel. Leipzig, 1856-61.
Blunck, Richard. *Friedrich Nietzsche: Kindheit und Jugend*. Munich and Basel, 1953.
Campbell, T. Moody. "Nietzsche – Wagner to 1872," *PMLA*, LVI (1941), 544-577.
Deiters, Hermann. *Johannes Brahms*. Leipzig: Breitkopf und Härtel, 1880.
Dippel, Paul Gerhardt. *Wagner und Nietzsche: Eine Untersuchung über Grundlagen und Motive ihrer Trennung*. Sprache und Dichtung, Vol. 54, Bern, 1934.
Ehlert, Ludwig. *Briefe über Musik an eine Freundin*. Berlin, 1859.
Förster-Nietzsche, Elisabeth. *Das Leben Friedrich Nietzsches*. 3 vols. Leipzig, 1895-1904.
– *Wagner und Nietzsche zur Zeit ihrer Freundschaft*. Munich, 1915.
Fortlage, Karl. *Das musikalische System der Griechen in seiner Urgestalt*. Leipzig, 1847.
Hanslick, Eduard. *Vom Musikalisch-Schönen: Ein Beitrag zur Revision der Aesthetik der Tonkunst*. 3d. ed., Leipzig, 1865.
Hueffer, Francis. *Richard Wagner and the Music of the Future*. London, 1874.
Jahn, Otto. *Gesammelte Aufsätze über Musik*. 2nd ed., Leipzig, 1867.
– *Wolfgang Amadeus Mozart*. 4 vols. Leipzig, 1856-59.
Krug, Gustav. *Vier Gesänge für eine Singstimme mit Pianofortebegleitung*. Leipzig: Breitkopf und Härtel, n. d.
Landmann, Michael. *Geist und Leben: Varia Nietzscheana*. Bonn, 1951.

LIST OF WORKS CITED

Lange, Friedrich Albert. *Geschichte des Materialismus und Kritik seiner Bedeutung in der Gegenwart.* 2 vols. Iserlohn, 1866.

Lenzewski, Gustav. "Nietzsche und Wagner," *Die Meistersinger von Nürnberg.* Programmheft der Bayreuther Festspiele 1959 (Bayreuth, 1959), pp. 18-27.

Marx, Adolf Bernhard. *Ludwig von Beethoven: Leben und Schaffen.* 2 vols. Berlin, 1859.

du Moulin-Eckart, Richard. *Cosima Wagner.* 2 vols. Munich, 1929-31.

Neue Zeitschrift für Musik, ed. Robert Schumann, Franz Brendel, *et al.*, Leipzig, 1834 ff.

Newman, Ernest. *The Life of Richard Wagner.* 4 vols. New York, 1933-46.

Nietzsche, Friedrich. *Werke.* 16 vols. Leipzig: C. G. Naumann, A. Kröner, 1901-11.

– *Werke und Briefe: Historisch-kritische Gesamtausgabe. Werke*, 5 vols. Munich: Oskar Beck, 1934-40. *Briefe*, 4 vols. Munich: Oskar Beck, 1938-42.

– *Werke in drei Bänden*, ed. Karl Schlechta. Munich: Carl Hanser, 1956.

– *Gesammelte Briefe.* 5 vols. Berlin and Leipzig, 1900-09.

– *Sokrates und die griechische Tragödie*, ed. Hans Joachim Mette. Siebente Jahresgabe der Gesellschaft der Freunde des Nietzsche-Archivs, Munich, 1933.

– *Hymnus an das Leben.* Leipzig: Fritzsch, 1887.

– *Musikalische Werke*, ed. Georg Göhler. Vol. I, Leipzig: Kistner und Siegel, 1924.

Oehler, Max, ed. *Nietzsches Bibliothek.* Vierzehnte Jahresgabe der Gesellschaft der Freunde des Nietzsche-Archivs, Weimar, 1942.

Reissmann, August. *Allgemeine Geschichte der Musik.* 3 vols. Munich, 1863-64.

– *Robert Schumann: Sein Leben und seine Werke.* Berlin, 1865.

LIST OF WORKS CITED

Schauffler, Robert H. *The Unknown Brahms*. New York, 1933.
Schopenhauer, Arthur. *Sämtliche Werke*, ed. Arthur Hübscher. 2nd ed., 7 vols. Wiesbaden, 1946-50.
Stein, Jack. *Richard Wagner and the Synthesis of the Arts*. Detroit, 1960.
Wagner, Richard. *Gesammelte Schriften und Dichtungen*. 10 vols. Leipzig: E. W. Fritzsch, 1871-83.
Westernhagen, Curt von. *Richard Wagner*. Zürich, 1956.
- "Nietzsche und die deutsche Musik," *Bayreuther Blätter*, LIX (1936), 8-18.
- "Wagner und Nietzsche," *Die Musik*, XXVIII, No. 10 (July, 1936), 725-731.

INDEX

Aeschylus, 17, 90.
Albrechtsberger, Johann Georg, 16, 19, 87.
Andler, Charles, 91.
Anregungen für Kunst, Leben und Wissenschaft, 15.
Bach, Johann Sebastian, 6, 7, 21, 35, 57f.
Bartók, Béla, 53.
Beethoven, Ludwig van, 6, 7, 8, 29, 31, 48, 57, 65, 90.
Berlioz, Hector, 7, 9, 32.
Bizet, Georges, 82.
Blunck, Richard, 85, 87.
Brahms, Johannes, 28, 32, 35, 74, 78, 81, 82, 92f.
Brendel, Franz, 14f.
Brockhaus, Hermann, 60, 61.
Brockhaus, Ottilie (Wagner's sister), 59f, 61.
Bülow, Hans v., 1, 12, 19, 64, 69, 73.

Campbell, T. Moody, 85, 86.
Chopin, Frédéric, 75, 82.
Cortot, Alfred, 91.

Deiters, Hermann, 33, 88.
Deussen, Paul, 40, 42.
Dippel, Paul Gerhardt, 91, 92.
Dürer, Albrecht, 60.

Ehlert, Ludwig, 55, 90.

Förster-Nietzsche, Elisabeth, vii, 2, 6, 7, 14, 29, 85, 91, 92.
Fortlage, Karl, 31, 88.

Gast, Peter, 82, 91, 92.
"Germania" (club), 9-15, 17, 18, 19, 20, 23, 25, 27, 28, 81.
Gersdorff, Carl v., 35, 39, 40, 77, 78.
Groth, Klaus, 28.

Handel, George Frederick, 4, 24, 81.
Hanslick, Eduard, vii, 32-34, 36, 47-49, 55f, 88, 89.
Haydn, Franz Joseph, 7, 8, 29.

Haym, Rudolf, 41f.
Hegel, Georg Wilhelm Friedrich, 15.
Hüffer, Franz (Francis Hueffer), 49f, 89.

Jahn, Otto, 33, 60f, 88, 90.

Kant, Immanuel, 41.
Kelterborn, Louis, 90f.
Krug, Gustav, 6, 7, 9, 11-15, 19, 21, 24, 27f, 30, 65, 73, 85, 86.
Krug, Gustav Adolph (father of the above), 6f, 12, 15.

Landmann, Michael, 39, 88.
Lange, Friedrich Albert, 41f, 44-46.
Lenzewski, Gustav, 85.
Lessing, Gotthold Ephraim, 34.
Levi, Hermann, 63.
Liszt, Franz, 7, 9, 26, 29, 32, 35, 91.

Marbach, Oswald, 54, 89f.
Marx, Adolf Bernhard, 31, 88.
Mendelssohn, Felix, 6, 7.
Meyerbeer, Giacomo, 35.
Monod, Gabriel, and Olga, *née* Herzen, 73, 91.
du Moulin-Eckart, Richard, 92.
Mozart, Wolfgang Amadeus, 7, 8, 29, 33, 82, 90.
Mushacke, Hermann, 40.

Neue Zeitschrift für Musik, 14f, 35, 52, 88, 89f.
Newman, Ernest, 28, 90, 91.
Nietzsche, Carl Ludwig (father), 4, 5.
Nietzsche, Carl Ludwig Joseph (brother), 4.
Nietzsche, Franziska (mother), 29, 38.
Nietzsche, Friedrich, *passim*.
    Works:
        "Fatum und Geschichte" (1862), 18.
        "Willensfreiheit und Fatum" (1862), 18.
        Essay on *Oedipus Rex* (1864), 17f, 87.

INDEX

Sokrates und die griechische Tragödie, 47, 88f.
Die Geburt der Tragödie, 17, 46f, 62, 65, 89, 90.
Schopenhauer als Erzieher, 37, 63.
Jenseits von Gut und Böse, 63.
Ecce homo, 1f, 15, 83.
Musical Compositions:
  "Miserere" (1860), 20.
  "Weihnachtsoratorium" (1860-61), 20, 87.
    "Einleitung und Chor", 21.
    "Einleitung zur Verkündigung Mariae", 22, 73.
    "Mariensverkündigung mit Fuge," 22.
    "Hirtenchor und Gesang des Mohren," 22.
    "Sternerwartung," 22f.
    "Der Könige Tod," 23.
  "Schmerz ist der Grundton der Natur" (1861), 23f.
  "Ermanarich" (1861-62), 25f, 70f.
  "Ungarische Skizzen" (1862), 27.
  "Große Sonate" (1863), 27.
  "Eine Sylvesternacht" (1863), 27, 68.
  Lieder (1861-66), 27f, 70.
    "Junge Fischerin," 29.
    "Kyrie" (1866), 68.
  "Nachklang einer Sylvesternacht..." (1871), 68-70, 72, 75, 80.
  "Manfred Meditation" (1872), 68, 69-73, 75, 76, 80.
  "Monodie à deux" (1873), 68, 73f.
  "Hymnus auf die Freundschaft" (1873), 68, 74-76, 77, 78f, 80, 92.
  "Hymnus auf die Einsamkeit" (?), 92.
  Hymnus an das Leben, 75, 85, 92.

Overbeck, Franz, 68f.

Palestrina, Giovanni Perluigi da, 20.
Petöfi, Sandor, 28.

Pinder, Wilhelm, 9, 11f, 15.
Pohl, Richard, 15.
Porges, Heinrich, 52.
Pushkin, Aleksander, 28.

Reissmann, August, 31, 88.
Ritschl, Friedrich, 31, 54f.
Ritschl, Sophie (wife of the above), 54f, 58, 61.
Rohde, Erwin, 1, 40f, 43, 51f, 54, 55, 59, 61, 62, 64.
Rossini, Gioacchino, 48, 57.
Rückert, Friedrich, 28.

Salomé, Lou, 75.
Schauffler, Robert H., 93.
Schloenbach, Arnold, 15.
Schopenhauer, Arthur, vii, 15, 17, 35, 37-49, 51f, 54, 56-64, 89.
Schubert, Franz, 6, 7, 29, 35, 82.
Schumann, Robert, 8, 13f, 28, 29, 31, 35, 75, 81.
Seyfried, Ignaz v., 19, 87.
Sophocles, 17, 87.
Stein, Jack, 87, 90.
Stravinsky, Igor, 53.
Strauss, David Friedrich, 83.

Ueberweg, Friedrich, 41.

Wagner, Cosima, 70, 90, 91.
Wagner, Richard, *passim*.
    Prose Works:
        Das Kunstwerk der Zukunft (1849), 85f.
        Oper und Drama (1851), 8, 16, 86.
        "Beethoven" (1870), 62, 89.
    Musical Works:
        Der fliegende Holländer, 65.
        Tannhäuser, 35, 60.
        Lohengrin, 60, 65, 90.

INDEX

Tristan und Isolde, 1, 2, 4, 12-14, 16, 18, 21, 22, 24, 27, 28, 35, 49, 52f, 55, 58, 64f, 67, 71, 72, 74, 81, 86f, 90.
Die Meistersinger von Nürnberg, 32, 51-56, 59, 61, 63, 81, 90.
Siegfried Idyll (1870), 90.
Kaisermarsch (1871), 90.
Der Ring des Nibelungen, 53, 66.
   Das Rheingold, 14.
   Die Walküre, 34f.
   Die Götterdämmerung, 66.
Parsifal, 23, 25.
Weber, Carl Maria v., 90.
Wenkel, Friedrich August, 40f.
Westernhagen, Curt v., 79f, 93.
Wolff, Hans M., 86, 87.

www.ingramcontent.com/pod-product-compliance
Lightning Source LLC
Chambersburg PA
CBHW031321150426
43191CB00005B/275